THE DEATH OF A
Dream

An athlete's journey to find a
passion-filled existence after athletics.

www.localpubco.com

Hanna Nuss

The Death of a Dream
Copyright © 2022 by Hanna Nuss

Published by Local. Pub. Co.
103 East Main Street
Denver, Iowa 50622
www.localpubco.com

Third Edition

Hardcover ISBN: 979-8-989-05092-5
Ebook ISBN: 979-8-9890509-4-9
Paperback ISBN: 978-1-234-56789-0

Library of Congress Catalog Number: 2024919630

The publisher is not responsible for websites (or their content) that are not owned by the publisher. The views and opinions expressed in this book are those of the author and do not necessarily reflect the official policy or position of the publisher.

For information about speaking engagements, bulk purchases, book signings, or media appearances, please contact
Local. Pub. Co. at:
speakers@localpubco.com
Phone: (319) 303-1017

Disclaimer
This book is a work of nonfiction. The names, events, and experiences detailed herein are presented as accurately as possible based on the author's recollection and available documentation. Some names and identifying details have been changed to protect the privacy of individuals. The author and publisher have made every effort to ensure the accuracy and completeness of the information in this book but assume no responsibility for errors or omissions.

The content of this book is intended for informational purposes only and should not be used as a substitute for professional advice. The views expressed herein are those of the author and do not necessarily reflect the views of the publisher.

Credits
Cover design by Katarina Nskvsky
Interior layout by Ruth Kokila
Photographs by Marcy Bergman

Trademarks
All product names, logos, and brands are property of their respective owners. Use of these names, logos, and brands does not imply endorsement.

DEDICATION

To my husband Jordan - the igniter of light and possibility.
You shall remain forever buried in my soul alongside the
unabating flame you relit. To one of the few souls on this
earth, I live to explore and spend eternity exploring with.
The world is infinitely ours.

TABLE OF CONTENTS

FOREWORD

*L*ooking back on a specific moment in time, while driving to Nashville with a group of girls, I now can see clearly what I missed in Hanna's journey. She talked about moving away – their recent road trip to Oregon, and their tentative plans to get out of Iowa. At the moment, it just seemed like another person looking to get out of our home state. But now, I see clearly, this was her searching. Searching for her true self. Searching for meaning. Searching for a place in this life.

Not too long after this trip, I started her podcast. I was a bit behind, so I got caught up and started to listen to every episode. I found something I always knew (through Hanna), that I love showing other people their potential and value in this world, and I was determined to be that person who kept Hanna going – to walk alongside her, until she bloomed and didn't "need" me anymore. Little did I know, her words would change the trajectory of my path. If you have ever heard of Jimmy Valvano, you may have heard these words from his famous 1993 ESPY speech, less than two months before his passing.

"To me there are three things everyone should do every day. Number one is to laugh. Number two is think – spend some time in thought. Number three, you should have your emotions move you to tears. If you laugh, think, and cry, that's a heck of a day." - Jimmy Valvano

Hanna's words did just that on many days. There is another saying that people come into your life for a reason, a season, or a lifetime. I have had people come into my life for reasons and seasons and have learned life changing lessons from them. In the past, Hanna and I were in each other's lives for seasons, but this time, this connection, it set us up to, what I only hope, is being part of each other's lives for a lifetime. In the early moments of us coming together, chatting via Messenger reflecting on her podcast, I don't believe we knew the impact we would have on each other.

Our journeys were so different, yet relatable. Her searching for meaning and value in her life, opening herself up to dream big, and leave the corporate world and become an entrepreneur. Me, on a journey to forgiveness for past trauma, manifesting my future, and turning my passion into a career. She was key to me being able to achieve these things in life, and without her, I wonder where I would be. We were there for each other through many beautiful no's, both in the present, and from our past.

This story of Hanna's, it's not just about someone finding their way in life and learning to dream again. It's about her journey. The journey many fear taking because we are afraid it will fail, or because we don't think it's possible. The journey some are ready to take, but others around them tell them they shouldn't. If there are a few things I have learned from Hanna, it's this...

Dream big and keep your eyes open. We all have dreams, and sometimes we shut those dreams down because we don't think our dreams are possible. Keep dreaming. And, keep your eyes open for the signs, because maybe what you thought you dreamt of, becomes something else you never saw coming. And if you're not paying attention, the opportunity may pass you by.

To be specific. I mean super specific. Make a list of your dreams. Whether that is your dream job, your dream house, your dream partner in life, your dream health, or whatever it is you want in life. Write it down. Keep reflecting on that list, make changes, add to it as you get closer and closer to getting what you want.

To celebrate your failures. Every single one of us has failures in life, some small, some large, some life changing. Being able to reflect upon those failures is important. In the moment of those failures, it's sometimes hard to see the lessons. Circle back to the things you feel you failed at – look at what you learned, what came out of that failure, and what came next. You may just see that that failure led to something even bigger and better.

And finally, to not let anyone tell you what's possible in your life.

So, what am I going to do now? Change the world.

Erika Brighi

INTRODUCTION

*T*hat moment when a dream dies seems rather swept under the rug to me. This realization would have a drastic impact on my life upon discovery four years ago.

It all started while sitting around a table with some newly found friends at dinner after a conference. We were reviewing takeaways from the day and exploring newfound thoughts and ideas. I sat nervous to go next. My voice shook, but I knew I was onto something I would not soon be able to shake. I looked down and then up again and said, "I realized that I stopped dreaming or dreamt too small after my dream of being a college athlete died."

Everyone sat there like I had just sucked the air out of the outdoor patio. Then one woman looked at me with alarmed acknowledgement and nodded. She felt the same way. It was as if we had both come into the world roaring and knowing exactly who we wanted to be, but when the wind picked up, we weren't given what we needed to withstand it.

Tragically, too often dreams die and blow away with the wind. I cannot see this moment swept under the rug anymore and see people showing up with an acceptance of less than because of it. I see parents comfort their children when the last moment happens. I fear what is said. As I know what society told me in that moment was untrue. The death of dreams is deserving of space and time to mourn. My request to the world is it stops simply moving on with the regular pace of life after dreams die.

This work is not for the faint of heart in self-discovery. This is for people ready to look their life in the eye and say it isn't good enough. This is for truth seekers and hope finders. This work is meant to walk alongside my journey from discovery to surrender. This work will lead us on a path to truth and put us on the road to that first step in faith. This is self-discovery done differently. This work is a rhythm and a story. The rhythm is life and the story is my truth.

I did everything society told me to do. I quit with silly childlike dreams of being a professional athlete. I got the degree, got married, bought the house, the car, had the kids, and got the steady job. I had even gone a little above and beyond all of that by the time I was twenty-eight. That was the age it all started to set in. I had this realization that there was a gaping hole that never seemed to be filled. That empty void sent me spiraling into a two-year time frame where I pushed everything I had to a new limit.

I chased success at the loss of everyone I knew and loved. In my mind, I felt like the void was just the fact that I hadn't "gotten there" yet, even though I couldn't even say where "there" was at that point.

So climb I did, taking down anyone and anything in my way. In some instances, getting where I believed the void would be filled, only to find a bigger void with a path of destruction leading to it now.

I found myself barely holding onto a life I didn't even know if I wanted. That was the void. No matter what I tried to fill it with, the result was always the same. Bigger void, more destruction to discovery. I was spiraling out of control. Nothing helped. I was everywhere and nowhere in my life. The dreamless path I was on was daunting, distracting, and damning.

Most people likely would have just laughed this off as a midlife crisis. In fact, most of those people I sought council in did. But that's the best way I could describe it. I had done it all and felt no better. I was continuing to climb and could see no light at the end of the tunnel.

The truth is, I look back now and realize what was missing, but at that time I thought the answer would just be to dream again. I thought the answer would just be to up the ante, work a little harder to take out bigger loans. But none of that had worked before, and I was determined to figure this out. It couldn't be as simple as writing new dreams down. My dream dying couldn't be a life sentence. I had to find my truth. I deserved to dream as big or as small as I saw fit. This was not according to society. This was going to be, for the first time, according to me.

I grew up in a town the size of most people's high schools. I always knew that I wanted to get out of my town, but not for the same reason most people do. Most people grow up wanting to leave small towns because they hate the entire experience. I wanted to leave because I loved it. I wanted to be the person the town could be proud to have known when she was little. I wanted to show everyone who looked like me that they could do it too.

I knew that a small town couldn't hold a space big enough for the life I could envision in 1994, and I loved that someday I would be the person this tiny town picked up on its shoulders and ran to the trophy. I knew this from a very young age. I just knew there were big things in store for me, as did my mother. Society was quick to point out all of the reasons I had no right dreaming that big in my town, with a population of less than 1,000, in a house on the main road which stretched less than a mile long end to end.

See this work, which I would love to tell you is about my journey to greatness and bigness that I had always forecasted, is the exact opposite. While I knew this from a young age, time and society clouded my knowledge. I was constantly reminded of my roots as something to hold me down to this toxic expectation of less than. I was born a big dreamer in a town where most dreams go to die. The projection of that was enough to beat senseless most of my early childhood audaciousness.

At the beginning of this work, I would start with surrendering to the fact that there was a very exact "line in the sand" moment where I started showing up as less and believing I was deserving of that as well.

What I didn't know was that as I continued, I would discover how deep the cut actually was. It was not enough to apply a band-aid and start dreaming again. I had to keep the cut open.

The first work was about sitting in the infection. As gross, dark, smelly, and terrifying as it may be. When we don't take time to sit with our reality, no matter how many times we bandage it, the cut reopens. I had done that too many times to count. I kept trying to carbon copy someone else's plan of what worked only to find myself back to my unmotivated, dreamless life, more lost and confused than ever.

It isn't worth just fixing it only to find a bend in the break down the road. This often appears as limiting beliefs that I could trick for a while, but would always rear their ugly heads, usually when least expected. When we find the source, we rediscover our truth. The truth that's always leading us back to love and acceptance of our entire being. We can't undo what is. We don't want to show up as anything but our truest existence.

We will walk through my experience, finding the root of all the things holding me back from the life I actually wanted to live. Deciding that we want to live life on our terms takes mustering up enough courage to rip off the band-aid, and then some more to open up the cut underneath.

The Death Of A Dream is a title written to save my soul and speak to yours.

It's a movement about coming back for the dreams that remain. Tapping back into this life and renouncing a comically miserable everyday experience. It's about rediscovering the person who moved through this world with passion and fire. My athlete self wants to tell us it isn't over even though that part was for me. I knowingly buried a part of myself the day I couldn't play sports anymore. I lost my only source of expression and expansion.

My hope is that this work releases the pressure of that moment. Had I never started this work, I would have been forever living as a partial being. My athlete self wants to tell us there is room for our full expression in this world. It doesn't only belong on that field, stage, court, or auditorium. We don't have to bury a piece of ourselves with our dream. We deserve to experience it all. Full person intact. In every piece of our daily existence. What happens to people who don't get to express themselves anymore? Well, I was still striving to find spotlights. There are just people who never feel whole without it. Those who find a separate spotlight probably go on living just fine. This is the best promise of a spotlight seeker's dream lived out: they get to remain involved in some way.

Those who can't find the right fit, maybe go on to live like me. Spiteful and ruthless in all attempts to knock anyone higher than them down, digging up drama anywhere and everywhere. My pent-up and unspent energy came out in bubbles just waiting to load and explode. I was "successful", but uncontrollable.

We should learn and accept this about successful people. They are capable of applying that skill of success to anything. My application looked like a degree in dream downgrading. Point and aim my rage at anyone daring to dream around me. I had a full comedy routine which made it seem whimsical and lighthearted (I promise you it wasn't).

If I couldn't live in full expression, neither could anyone around me, and I was a fearless competitor. I actually loved dreams prior to my dream dying, but I was using my dark experience to expand my darkness. That is what often happens with unspent and underutilized potential. I didn't know what to do with the energy I used to have an outlet for.

There's still use for that person in this world. I had told myself that dreams die and that's life. That person belonged on a volleyball court and life doesn't require that kind of fire, but it does.

Let this work be a callback to remembering the greatness that exists in each of us. Let it light a path back to the moment when we blew out the light reminding us who and what we know to be true. Greatness doesn't leave us when the dream dies. It strengthens our becoming, leading us to a new even truer experience. We're meant to rise. We're all meant to experience the greatness this life can offer. It's not just for a few. It's meant for all of us. It's meant for exactly where we find ourselves in our story today.

Parts of this work will shed light and share stories to get real with the person you have shown up as since. It hurts to write those words now considering how much dreams give me life. I find that's painfully often where our hate shows up most. Exactly where we were supposed to heal. Where the wound lies open.

In 2019, I gave myself a word. This is a pretty common self-help practice, so this doesn't originate with this work. That word was intention. I didn't adopt this word method until about mid-year. This was around the time that I would start this work. I knew only one thing at that point: I was tired. I was tired of operating in extreme highs and devastating lows. I used that word to set my focus point of success. Up until that point, everything I had done had been aimed at success that I left rather undefined, but always revolved around money equaling worth.

That's part of the middle-class mindset I was raised in. Everything I did was only worthy of pursuit if it was going to be financially fruitful. This isn't a terrible measure so long as it isn't adopted as the only way to provide worth in this world. But for me, that was it. Nothing was worth doing unless it produced positive cash flow. I had no hobbies. I had no friends I spent time with. I had no fun. I had limited happiness which always resulted in a sustaining feeling of guilt. I had work and free time, and most of my free time at that point was being filled with more work.

Intention guided me for the first time to a place of finding worth in things that brought me joy.

Intentionally moving through this world would bring me to a place of a steadier happiness than I had gotten used to feeling. The word brought freedom to my movements. It was the first time in my life that success boiled down to intention versus worth. Whatever I did, I had to do with intention. Which brought me to more silence than I had ever explored in my life. I had to think things over. I couldn't run too fast to see. This way of operating felt uncomfortable, but aligned with what I needed in that moment. Intention carved a path for my new way of existing and seeing worth in things that expanded my being.

This movement is about the understanding phases in life. This work closes with knowing of what is coming next so there's a newfound comfort exploring all the light and expansion.

While I was actively researching the phases, through this work, I found the repetitive nature of life navigation divine. What I wish I had known at my mid-life crisis(ish) was that it isn't all that spectacular. That life is a constant upgrade and understanding. This is usually the line between a societal norm experience and a spiritual one.

So, imagine a life always looking for a purpose. Some people find it "easily" and they tend to get labeled as "the gifted ones". While others stumble, fall, and give up on a life free of constant misery and the mundane. Those who find it early continue to upgrade their experience and continue expanding (usually finding more abundance than they know what to do with). They realize this simple fact. As long as they continue getting up, they will always land back on their feet.

Phase one explores the realization. This work will guide us to not jump off the deep end in this phase like I may or may have not done every time I approached this moment. This is the moment we realize this isn't it or this isn't going to happen.

Phase two is rage. This experience isn't fitting and everyone/everything is the cause. Nothing can save you here. I believe this phase is the result of unspent energy that has been lying stagnant for too long.

I bounced between phase one and phase two for a majority of my adult years. My passion usually turned into rage bubbling up at anyone and everyone, and once expelled I felt better for a while. The inability to channel passion in a positive way always returned me to the top.

These phases remind me of Mario (I didn't have a gaming counsel, but when we went to my cousin's I would watch). Life is always working to advance to the next level; but there are mushrooms and stars and ledges that stop us, take us to the next level, or return us to the very beginning.

When I started creating or giving my rage purpose, I would begin my first journey upward. The dangerous highs and lows of navigating that much of the time in rage mode is enough to drain everything you have.

I lived my life constantly looking for places to expel that excess energy I was no longer burning on a court. I found it, and when I couldn't find something to be mad at or someone to take it all out on...I created it. Drama followed me around like a puppy because drama always had the need for passion. It had a need for who I used to be and usually left me as the person taking a way too drastic opinion on small things, like what sides needed to be brought to Thanksgiving dinner.

Once I began writing, podcasting and exploring creative outlets for my excess energy, I moved into phase three. I also began a much less dramatic approach to life.

Phase three was ego check time. Which is and likely isn't what we know it to be. My ego had to find a back seat, which also meant my passion did too. I had been seeking a spotlight for so long that I had a lot of fear I would be unseen here. If I didn't bring the drama, I would disappear and I would be left unseen and passionless again. But this phase led me to listen and learn for the first time in my life. Which sent me into a deep self-discovery and accountability period.

Phase three is easy to avoid and stay checked out of forever because, again, it's looking at the reflection of who we are really showing up as. This isn't just getting to know an enneagram or any other personality test (I recommend them all, but enneagram is my main jam). This is stepping into an accountability agreement with yourself that may have never before been explored. This is the part where we renounce a scared and victim-filled narrative. We start a path back to our truth in this phase, while it's not an unscathed one, it is our truth.

In phase three, we begin to gain a deeper knowledge of ourselves and begin exploring our new terms. This is where the work will leave us, as this was the end of my first season. While the destination wasn't hard to pick, the acceptance of that being a potential reality is the work that was embarked on next.

This is self-development in the being, not the doing. Early on, I was lost enough to think this work was about what I did in this world. This is reflected in my daily podcast journal entries. I have come to know it's about who I am in this world, which can be a very complicated mission.

We'll start with the doing so we can understand the being. Being comes from the expansion of our full selves in this world. Since it takes a lot of doing to understand expansion, that's where we'll start. We have to get there with action even though the action is rather unimportant.

Over time, we'll be guided to a new and more peaceful knowing in our being. It all takes time. There's no quick fix meditation, diet, exercise, or journal session that can save us from the work. It will take daily showing up and checking in as we navigate our way back to ourselves. We can't force it. So as hard as this will be for some of us to accept, we must tread lightly and lovingly into the work of self-discovery and true dreams with a knowing pace of acceptance and flow. I find this applicable to all things.

I've always wanted to write words. I've always wanted to speak words. I just got busy living a life I prescribed myself in acceptance of my smallness, unknowingly brought on by my dream's death.

You should know that every morning before I record my podcast, I repeat this mantra three times. "I am given the words that find the ears ready to receive." So, if you are still reading, this work contains words that you are ready to receive.

CHAPTER ONE

THE MOVEMENT

CHAPTER ONE

This Isn't Me

Pain is pain.

This was not meant to be a story. This was and is just my life.

I started recording what would play out over the last four years, but the story started in a spiral. While the show recorded a portion of that spiral still happening, this explains the tipping point. These moments prior to pushing record were the moments where I decided to start figuring this out.

Many things happened to propel this work forward, but this was the moment where I would never be the same. I find it most important to speak to you for this reason and this reason alone.

Nothing you will read here is that abnormal or detrimental. People all over the world have worse wake up calls. I was still suffering. I was still operating as less, and so maybe this story will give you permission to examine your own life.

It doesn't have to be all that painful compared to the world. The pain is yours, as is the story. There is no comparison. What hurts is worthy of intentional exploration. The significance doesn't have to fit a specific scale. What is traumatic is ours. What is painful is ours, too. We can explore anywhere pain exists no matter the "normalcy" of it in the human experience.

Pain is deserving of exploration, not just pain compared to others. I want to make sure to point that out because we may nod and think as we read these stories that it isn't that bad, but I didn't write this for sympathy or with any intention of having it worse than anyone else in this world. I wrote it to create prompts that create exploration. I wrote it to let us all know that no matter the significance to the world, we deserve our own validation of the need to heal from what hurt us.

I can't make us all look at it this way, but I will continue to pen my story in hopes it prompts you to examine your own. To look for pain that may have been shrugged off because it "wasn't that bad." That pain is where we find some of our first clues to what is holding us back.

Snowy Day.

My kids and I had just come in from playing outside on a cold, snowy day.

We were making our way into the house, stripping off layers and placing them on heat registers to dry. I looked back at the wreckage of our short-lived outdoor bliss. My eyes moved to the living room, which was always an unexplainable mess, to the endless loads of laundry piled up on my path, to the unvacuumed carpet. All of this was surrounded by the ominous smell of dishes piled so high I couldn't even begin to explore.

I walked into the dining room and it was as if everything had taken up residence in my brain and nothing more could fit. Everything I had left came boiling over at that very moment. You know when people say they saw red? This was that for me.

It was February 2019. I had started the year with a promise to myself and my husband that this necessary laptop purchase would be worth it. It would finally allow me to write. At that point, it was just easier to place blame and responsibility on something tangible. The computer was the problem.

Yet, every time I would look at the computer, I would start back down the path of blame once again. What boiled over at that moment was the fact that writing was supposed to save me and nothing was flowing with nothing on the horizon. It was the realization that I had gotten it wrong. The excitement to explore something new, exciting, and challenging had worn off yet again!

I must have appeared manic because my five-year-old came bouncing in with her two-year-old sister to see me in this mental state of spinning only to say, "Mom, we're hungry," followed with, "Are you okay?"

I must not have processed the "are you okay" because I came unglued. I ripped the American Girl Doll high chair off the table, threw it across the room, and just screamed. It wasn't a scream of fear. It was a scream of all the anger in my body releasing at once. It felt as though my entire body was set on fire. I started shaking and crying. My head was unable to process anything else in the world.

At that exact moment, I remember going limp and found it hard to move. Laying curled up in a ball was the only thing that felt right. My five-year-old came to my rescue and helped me limp up to my room. I whaled uninterrupted for what felt like hours. When my two-year-old wandered up to hug me, I knew it was time to rejoin the world of the living. I found my way back to the same mess that had sent me spiraling just a short while ago. I found myself struggling to accept the life I had. This was made even more complicated by the fact that everything from the outside looked better than fine.

According to the everyday interpretation of the American dream, I had arrived. I had children being raised by home-owning, college-educated parents, in a rural bedroom community. We were both making more than our parents were at our age, so by most standard measures we were living the picture-perfect vision of a picture-perfect life.

As hard as I tried to pinpoint it and uncover a reason for my discontent, a place to point the finger, I was coming up listless. Great husband, great kids, and what seemed like an entire life gone wrong leading up to everything going right.

Doctor's Office.

It was shortly after that day that I sent myself into my midwife's office. Surely the hormones were to blame for this deep burning anger inside of me.

I sat on the paper-lined exam table, uncomfortably knowing I was about to admit the one secret I had been working so hard to cover up. I wasn't satisfied with my life and I had every reason in the world to be.

Even worse, I was about to admit that I had been able to bottle it up until now, but it kept bubbling over at all the wrong times. I was certain motherhood or womanhood was to blame. I found myself kind of hoping that I had some sort of complex medical condition that was complicated, but curable so there was something to point a finger at.

I sat nervously fidgeting with the paper underneath me. I breezed my way through the normal questions: allergies, surgeries, weight, and height. Then tension built in the room and I could feel my heart beating out of my chest. The room went quiet and the midwife swiveled her chair away from her computer and asked, "So what are we seeing you for today?"

I cleared my thoughts and tried to calm myself before I spoke. It didn't work. There it was again, the bubbling followed by the spiraling. Every word rushed out of my body as if they were afraid to get stuck and remain unseen. I couldn't have stopped talking if I wanted to.

My midwife kindly stopped the spiral. By the third time around the loop, I suppose she had heard enough. It felt as if my world had shattered twice that week. Here I sat exposed in a weird hospital gown from the late eighties, pouring out my heart to someone who had known me for all of two minutes. When she stopped me, I remember not knowing if I even could, but I did.

She seemed rather unalarmed and said plainly, "You are not alone."

I think she expected this to make me feel better, but it only set off more anger alarms than before. I thought, What?!? I'm not alone in this, but I've never heard of anyone struggling with this before. How can this be?

She would go on to explain that hormones and the ups and downs are a rather regular part of motherhood and a woman's experience. She suggested a rather mild anti-anxiety medication to get me through the spirals, anxiety, and extreme lows.

I told her I would have to think about it. I left that office more lost than found. I don't remember the exact reason, but I knew this was important for me to experience and figure out. I remember telling no one. I couldn't fathom attempting to recount the shocking reality of this moment and the need for medication among mothers my age. It was best to keep the secret close to my chest like I had been taught my entire life. Keep it together. Look the part and don't let it boil over. Keep it close. People don't need your darkness. I had kept the hate for my life locked up tight since the moment I last walked off a gym floor.

This wasn't motherhood, it was bigger than that. In that office, all I could admit was the easy anxieties, the obvious reason for the boil over. I couldn't bring myself to admit the real reason. The fact that every day I committed to this life of small-town motherhood was another day and step away from the life I knew I was supposed to live.

It wasn't motherhood, but that was the easier blame for people to accept. Not that I would ever admit that to anyone outside of a doctor's appointment. No one could know that somewhere swimming inside my life was an unease and an alarming disappointment that kept me awake at night. It was supposed to be bigger than this. It was supposed to be more. I had more than saving for college funds and retirement on my list of things to do.

Everything was wonderful and I was still suffocating. Everything was on track and I was still suffering. Nothing all that wrong and most things just right, and yet I felt this rising anger building with each breath. The buildup which boiled over that winter day. I knew somewhere deep inside of me that medicating and continuing to push down this feeling would only lead me back here again.

I was left with nothing but another overwhelming example of my failure to maintain a home and a five-year-old's fearful pat on my shoulder with a loving whisper, "Mommy, you'll be okay."

Every moment before that day and the day at the doctor's office, I had been able to contain it, bury it, leave it all unexpressed. But the boiling worsened. The need to numb became a relentless part of my never-ending to-do list.

Numb

Since I was a rural Midwestern mother, I didn't turn to anything all that scary for the numbing. I was "good." I had normalized solutions for distractions from this feeling. One of those being shopping. Spending most of my free time filling my house with things I "needed," most of which I most certainly did not.

Another being food. Since I was thin privileged, no one seemed concerned about that either. I would spend the occasional night out drinking a little too much. These were normal solutions, nothing to be concerned about. In fact, where I come from, these things are so normal it's as if most adult friend groups' way of relating to one another are dependent on the activity of the above three things. This is not a problem either, but it was a problem for me. I was growing more and more dependent on these activities. It was more than trying to fit in a social circle. I had to have them in my life or I was at risk of boiling over once again.

So anywhere I couldn't fill the gap with these activities, I filled with work. Yet another rather non-concerning addiction. My schedule was so packed that I couldn't think if I wanted to. Downtime did not exist. It simply couldn't if I was going to survive my own mind. That left me as a mere pawn in my own life. I was nothing. I was everywhere and nowhere at all. Resisting an existence I knew I deserved but kept stealing from myself. I feared letting the silence in. I feared who I was when the light went down on the day. At night, it was just me and my mind. My mind was unrelenting in its awareness that there was something missing. I feared that someday I would no longer be able to drown out the silence with these coping mechanisms, and I would be spiraling and searching for something more to fill the void. To find something more fitting and truer to the place where my purpose was supposed to be. The less these things seemed to curb this fear, the worse it got. The more I needed, the less I found.

Whisper

I knew somewhere deep inside me was more than what I was living. During this time, a whisper made its way to a yell, which made drowning out the noise all the more important. That whisper had always been confirming my life's work and my alignment with it. It always said to change lives. I always responded with my marketed pitch for how this given line of work fit that mold. Each time the whisper came back, I would know it was time for something new. This was the first time I didn't cater to the whisper. I didn't continue convincing it I was right. I just went right on living.

I didn't know what change was to be made from here. I had done it all. I set goals and reached them, and now I figured this was the time that people like me settled in, so I ignored it. The more I ignored it and filled in the gaps, the louder it yelled.

I like to call this part the resisting pain portion of this work. I knew it was calling me to change and yet I ran. All that running led me straight into pain not meant for me. I could have redirected at the soft whisper, but I insisted comfort was better than the pain of figuring out what came next.

I refer to my whisper as this guiding voice. I've heard not everyone has this. I don't believe that. I believe not everyone listens, learns, and relies on it, but we all have it. Our intuition or gut instinct.

Once the whisper became a yell, it started showing up in new ways, likely because I ignored it. Finding ways to me even in my unconscious states. Once a week for that entire year, I would wake up from the same nightmare. In my dream I would be getting robbed, abducted, or something else terrifying, and every time I started to scream, nothing would come out. The moment I would wake up, everything would disappear, but the fear and the knowledge that this was bigger than just an average nightmare remained. What was it about my voiceless dream that it kept coming back?

The scream was non-existent. Normally my husband would end up waking me up from this nightmare, because even though I wasn't screaming in the dream, I was making very strange straining sounds in real life.

There was something about the frequency of the whisper increasing in volume and the nightmares happening. There are usually clues, little voices, or signals that advance us in our work on this planet. While mine had become quite scary and almost threatening, they were always there to guide me to make the next choice.

The resistance caused the change in the approach. This was no longer a marketable change in life. It was going to require a distinct change in vibration. The universe would not let me continue to say I hated my life and keep living the same way no matter how bad I tried. The discomfort was too great. The yelling was what had sent me spinning that snowy day. I could no longer deny what I knew, and I knew I wanted something different.

The discomfort was forced, but necessary for action that wouldn't have taken otherwise. I look for this now prior to the point of pain. Always looking for ways to trust the intuition that's always guiding me to my highest point. No one knows the hum underneath our outward appearance. Only we do. Only we know when something has reached its limit, and only we know our way back.

This work isn't just to get you to dream again. It's also to get you to listen. The dream is the action, it's tangible, and listening is the beginning. It's the higher understanding of self and how the world is guiding our path. My whisper has always been in my best interest. My ego sometimes only wants to stick to the plan. Stick to the comfortable. Stick to the knowing.

I still find that my intuition always knows the next right move. The more I leaned on it and trusted it, the more willing it was to speak up at all times. It used to only intervene when redirection was needed. Now it guides everything. I no longer like to exist in a world where intuition doesn't guide my movements. It was just there to push me past my ego and now it is everywhere.

I like a life where I love how my body, mind, spirit, and soul all play together to make the world go round. It's a whole and beautiful way to experience this world. I used to attempt to sway my whisper to guide me to where my ego was comfortable. Now

I let it guide me to places I have never been. Every day reaching new heights and experiencing new norms. Our life journey meant to twist and turn, our soul's purpose meant to guide us unwavering. This is about love of who the universe has made you to be, inner guidance and all.

It's not

This movement is not about some "suck it up and get over it" strategies to make your way back to loving your life. While there are moments for leadership like that, in my experience this is not one. This moment is about accepting and learning to trust a guidance system society has taught us to ignore. This moment is about finding our place in activities where the energy repeats and motivation is not needed.

Remember when we failed through life unapologetically, always letting what feels the best guide us? I do. I was six. Most days I could be found rummaging around town on an old railroad track that ran behind my house. I would explore until the world went to bed, and I was excited to wake up with a new world to explore each day. It was likely rather uninteresting, but I found it fascinating. Everything about it. I could imagine what life was like when trains ran through this town. I could imagine what an abandoned building was being used for, or what I would use it for if it were mine. I could wander and wonder all day long with boredom at bay. I would spend my days exploring, not a care in the world.

Now I know this is hard to take given we all have responsibilities to tend to and mouths to feed, but can we just for a second remember that free feeling? The wind in our hair. The adventure all around us. That is a feeling we want to get back to. The guidance that told us what to explore next or told us to jump or giggle uncontrollably. Maybe that's what's lost. Maybe we all lost our knowledge and came to depend on our intuition only in scary situations, but it used to guide us in light too. It was the only way we knew how to make decisions and it didn't leave us. This work is about discovering that truth and that whisper. It's about making a nod to the true and uncomfortable ways that our lives play out sometimes. The movement is about you finding you in your life again.

CHAPTER TWO
The Dream

D-1

Division One athlete. To this day, I can't stress how meaningful I thought that experience would have been to me. I propped it up as the highest level a human on this earth could attain (I realize that is ridiculous). To me, division one athletes were godlike. It meant that person made it. That person was seen as important, valid, and was wanted by more than just the community.

For me, it was about breaking free and being bigger than what was right in front of me. I don't actually know why. I think for me it was just about scale. If I was going to be something, do something, or go somewhere, I wasn't wasting my time with the small stuff. I was going big or going home.

Since I was a tall kid, this was an easy dream to assign, and assign people did. At all grocery stores, doctor offices, and, well, everywhere my height was noticed, usually followed up with an "I hope you play basketball."

That was enough for me. People seeing me as something more than I could see? Sign me up. What was it that you said about basketball? I am all in. I shot hoops in the driveway, went to all open gyms, got on travel teams, and went after this goal of mine. Basketball posters lined my room. Rebecca Lobo and Vince Carter were my idols. I had even picked the school. Michigan was it for me. I have not the slightest idea why, yet that was where I was going to get my full ride division one basketball scholarship.

By seventh grade, I decided that was going to be my life. I would ride this sport people had told me my whole life I should be good at all the way to the pearly gates. No need for a game plan.

The plan: division one athlete. The school: Michigan. The sport: basketball.

The Bet

There I was, a string bean of a kid standing outside my aunt and uncle's pool one summer. Bony body dripping with chlorine and confidence. I had shot up to around five foot eight in the last month. Conversations around my talent and work ethic were always floating around, but that day's conversation had pulled me out of the pool.

My dad and uncle were grilling, likely discussing a game I had played, and they had brought up college sports. My dad always had Iowa Hawkeye basketball on the TV when we were kids, likely a habit he learned from his grandma, who played on one of Iowa's first female high school basketball teams and loved sports. So, I looked up to those players without really ever understanding what being an athlete at that level meant. For me, it meant attention, big stages, television, and on this day, the stakes were raised even higher.

That day, I told my dad and my uncle that one day I would be on TV playing basketball. I told them that I would be better than the people they watch on TV. So, my dad wagered a bet. Staring at his skinny stick of a kid, I'm sure he knew it would be a bet he would never have to make good on. He said, "Okay, I'll tell you what. You get a full ride division-one scholarship to play, I'll send you to school in your dream car."

We shook hands and that young day division athlete had received even more fire behind her than she ever had before.

Ford Mustang

What was the car, you might be wondering. I have no idea why the obsession. My family was never that into cars, so the fact that I had a dream car (like enough to have posters of it up in my room) in seventh grade is a little strange, but what can I say...I wear my decisions and obsessions like a suit of armor. A 1998 Ford Mustang GT Convertible- Bright Yellow. Black leather interior, tape player, and six disk CD player. I didn't know if I wanted the college scholarship or the car more, but it didn't really matter. I could already feel my hair whipping in the wind driving up to Michigan. Posters in my room made it even easier to feel like a dream coming true. Basketball camps and team opportunities kept on coming up. There was no doubt I was going to win that bet.

My eighth-grade winter, I was introduced to volleyball for the first time as something I would be "great at." Honestly, in eighth grade I found the game really boring, no rally scoring and middle school coaching likely fueled the distaste.

That year, a new volleyball coach had taken over the program, and although I didn't feel that impact during the middle school season, I was being coaxed to come try out for this new AAU thing that winter. My attendance was dependent on kids in my class wanting to go, so I went and entertained the idea that volleyball could "be fun" to play.

Following my tryout, numerous calls were made to my parents (thank you to my coaches Joe, Barry, and Brian, who fought for something none of us could see) who didn't care one way or the other as long as they didn't have to pay the fees.

The coach convinced all of us that volleyball could be my thing. I kept telling him basketball was, but it felt good to be wanted. My first time playing, I played middle blocker. It made sense, I was five foot ten and in eighth grade. The first time I got a block, it was over. It had to be this sport. The world was going to have to be okay with my switch. After a quick AAU season, I found myself starting as a freshman about eight months into my career. I didn't even know much, but who I became was fully engaged in that game, I couldn't recognize. It was as if every practice and game I floated above my being for spurts of time. So there was a slight shift in the dream but the car, bet, and laser-like focus remained the same.

The plan: division one athlete. The school: Michigan. The sport: volleyball.

Volleyball

I couldn't give up on this. Not with the way I felt when I played. Most kids gave it up, but I couldn't do it. I remember standing in the line at my graduation party (sorry to anyone who attended. I took that graduation money and ran. Thank you's falling quickly off the to-do list. Consider this your long-awaited thank you). There I stood, shaking hands and having to explain to almost every person inquiring that volleyball was the plan. People wanted more from me, a firmer answer, a major, or at least parents who made me come up with a lie, but that wasn't the reality. I was blissfully unaware and loving that my dream was still alive. Maybe just maybe I was running from a reality I never wanted brought to my awareness. The fact that this all would end never even crossed my mind.

Still, it wasn't responsible for an eighteen-year-old to not have a planned exit. But I didn't. I hadn't given my next move even the slightest thought. By my senior year, the plan shifted a bit, but even given a slight detour, I could still see the train on the track. I had gotten picked up by a successful division-two junior college my senior year by a coach who would forever change my life.

Coaches are it for me. I still remain unsure of what she saw in the arrogant and blissfully ignorant athlete I was, but I am thankful she found something. Junior college still meant two years to train, improve, and get that scholarship. My dad got me a settle car. It was no Mustang he would say, but my scholarship was no division one scholarship either, so we both shook hands on a salvaged green chevy malibu and a partial junior college scholarship. It seemed okay to settle there because this was only a stepping stone to better connect me with what I wanted.

The plan: division one athlete. The school: Michigan. The sport: volleyball.

Doctor

After the dust settled on my life, somewhere after the excitement of becoming an adult wore off, I would start looking back at my roots for a source of inspiration. Before the athletic dreams, I would wonder, "What do I want?"

I could remember my mom always telling people I was going to be a doctor. She talked about it so much I didn't have the heart to tell her it had changed. I felt bad forcing her to rehearse a new line about me. "Hanna wants to be a doctor because she spent so much of her life in and out of hospitals," she would say. Even though I did want to be a doctor when I was little, I couldn't pinpoint where that fell off or why it changed to being an athlete.

I was forced to dig deeper. A lot of this Death Of A Dream work is related in some way to my past learnings of who I was and how I got here. The work took a lot of patience in the process of the pursuit. It wasn't just written down somewhere. The memories were foggy at this point and as hard as I tried, some I just couldn't see. There are still pieces that remain in the fog, but I have found the two dreams I had growing up.

The first dream before the athletic visions was to be a doctor. I know my mom told people that it was because of my utopian childhood in and out of hospitals, but upon the lifting of the fog, I remembered. It was about the money. One of the richest, most eclectic and eccentric humans I had ever been lucky enough to meet was my great grandpa's doctor. Doctor Bickley.

He was a tiny man who wore the most adorable bow tie. His entire office was decorated with knick knacks he collected from all over the world.

I don't know why it impressed me so much. I suppose it was that I had never left the area I was born in and neither had anyone I knew. So someone exploring the entire world right in front of me was enough reason to stand at attention, take notes, and maybe aspire to be like that.

While I couldn't have likely communicated that I wanted to be a doctor because I wanted to be rich enough to explore the world, that was it. Yeah, healing the sick seemed like a cool side project, but funds, which were always communicated as in short supply at my house, were the ticket to the freedom I desired. I want to point out that being raised in a scarce household can spoil the drinking water of dreams. I wasn't chasing a passion as much as I was chasing a lifestyle which I assigned to a certain income bracket, not something I genuinely wanted to do. Regardless of the reason, that was the dream.

Yellow Hanes Sweatsuit

Some might read all of this and think "how unfortunate" or "where were her parents." You should know the mixture of my mind and my parents' parenting style was a beautiful thing. They never stopped me from believing and exploring anything. It may have been the fact that I was the third child. They let me be. They let me be me. My mom noticed my originality early on and supported it. She may have gone a little hard supporting it. So much that I spent summers riding around town on a yellow banana seat bike in a yellow Hanes cut off sweatsuit that my mom fabric crayoned Hanna Banana on. I am the most. I suppose I always have been. Along with my affinity for yellow, I would put my short hair up in about twenty tiny ponytails. I am attempting to paint a picture you likely can't imagine. Tall. Thin. String bean of a kid. Strawberry blonde hair. Cut into basically a girl version of a bowl cut. Front teeth gapped. Freckle cheeked ball of constant energy. Most babysitters lovingly passed on the nickname Hammer Hanna. Kicked out of a lot of dinner tables for laughing uncontrollably. My energy and identity were so known, strong, and sure. I didn't have a care in the world. I was always sure that I was going to be whatever I wanted. I was going to do whatever I wanted. I was also always told that I did not care what anyone thought. Can you imagine a kid like that? Can you imagine what a human like that could do in this world?

I knew nothing of the rarity of my intrepid confidence. Had not a clue in this world of my parents protecting that and allowing me to grow up in that bubble of belief was aligned with my ability to survive as a soul driven human for as long as I did.

My heart was always placed boldly in belief on my sleeve. There are days when I feel that distinct human rise from the ground. I had buried her so long ago it has taken time, energy, and patience to feel her in her fullness. That energy still wavers and I don't know if I'll ever feel my full power consistently again, but I know I feel her more and more with each passing day doing this work. I was born and raised a big dreamer and believer. A wild creative with intrinsic gifts. I was blessed to explore my creativity with everything. My clothing was vibrant and an interesting mix of mostly hand-me-downs that I had a knack for constantly outgrowing. My room walls were yellow underneath a collage of things I found beautiful in this world. Creativity was taken off the table as a dream for me before I could even offer it into existence.

Art, music, dance, or theater just weren't things someone like me should put time into pursuing. I think those paths would have been extremely fitting given my love of orchestrating shows with my little brother and my constant interest in every opportunity to perform in public. That I knew for sure could never be. Creativity as a career. Not here. Not you. Not now. Not then. Not ever again. It was fun to do, but it wasn't a realistic money making, family feeding path. I knew that early enough to not even bother bringing it up. It wasn't all that crazy. Most of my family, excluding all of my siblings, but including my mom and her siblings, were extremely artistic. No one ever really made it a career, but when they needed those skills, they could always drum someone up to deliver. It's weird to me that somewhere something gets spoken of or off handedly remarked and for whatever reason it sticks like glue. Making its way into our core memories and finding a way to take up space forever. I can't find this one anywhere. I'm unsure where it came from. Maybe this was placed so early on that the memory no longer exists, maybe I just adopted it as an inherent truth.

More than a game

Creatively expressing things and imagining in my youth integrated perfectly to a career in athletics. I loved how games required relentless optimism and synergy of a group of people all believing in the same thing at the same time. Optimism that would keep me in coaches' offices imagining what could be.

I had this way of seeing things further than most people. This ability to always paint the picture back to the original plan. My coaches must have needed to see the way I looked at the world and navigated competition or they couldn't get rid of me if they tried because I was always in their offices. I always saw it as a win. Even in moments where it wasn't working the way I thought it would, I always found a way to sow a silver lining. Bringing coaches, teammates, and fans back in no matter the situation was my favorite part.

It's hard to tell now whether or not I loved the game or the art that was keeping everyone on the same chapter. I also loved the way bodies, equipment, play surface, coaches, players, and fans all found harmony making this thing for people to care about. To love. Sports were like a symphony to me. I loved closing my eyes and feeling the game arrive. Also, pep band. Enough said. The whistles, squeaks, and movement were enough to steal the breath of all of my days.

I could watch nothing and still feel who won. Team chemistry ringing out like a bell in energetic vibrations. I would sit and obsess about it for hours. I loved the art of sports more than anything. The team, the synergy, the creation of common goals, visions, and dreams.

Maybe it was the openness of dreaming in sports as well. Goals were always in unison and shared openly like nowhere I had ever experienced. Sports require more imagination and creativity than most give them credit for. I loved moving my dream and creativity to the athletic space. While the path was even narrower, for whatever reason people believed in that and in me doing that. Art...not so much. Sports...absolutely limitless. An unknown art. An expression of beauty, energy, and synergy.

When I think about the roots of those dreams, I think a lot about how much of it I actually decided and how much of it was based on scarce ideologies of the world that were forced on me since as early as infancy. There was always a plan to get out and explore my list of to-dos. I knew that my tiny town was important, but would never be able to hold the bigness of me forever.

Even though I knew I wanted out, I also wanted to be the person everyone was proud to know in that tiny town, and most importantly, the proof point for dreamers like me that you can do it if you put your mind to it. The run to the trophy moment always played in the background of me knowing I would leave. I was always dreaming of this even when I scored fifty cents and got to walk down to John's convenience store to buy my brother and me Tootsie Pops. Hoping to get the Indian with the arrow and star to turn in for another sucker. I still don't know if that was a thing or if the attendant just felt bad for us, but I still think it was a thing.

Even though no one really told me I couldn't be these things or dream this big, I still always felt this unnerving wave of unexplainable energy around me and my bold, dreaming self. Like I was just lucky enough to float above all these people who couldn't or didn't.

I thought I would just go on floating like that forever. Honestly, the athlete route seemed more realistic because I actually knew people who had left this little town to play sports. I didn't know them, but I heard stories about them. People would always talk about how they knew so-and-so back in the day. I think about that a lot when I drive through small towns. How many of these kids shooting hoops under a street light are dreaming of the day when this dream carries them away from there like I did? It just made more sense to me.

People had confirmed athletics as a possible route for me. No one apart from my mom did that for the doctor dream, and I didn't know of anyone that had become a doctor. Not because they didn't exist, just because it wasn't talked about as much. So, athlete became the chosen path. I just couldn't see beyond what I was told to be. Lower middle class, partially college educated parents, midwestern, in a tiny town with no good reason to believe I could ever be anything more.

All I had was a dream that would never count for dot points on a resume.

CHAPTER THREE

The Death

Parking Lot

It was a normal day much like any other. I was standing outside in the parking lot of my apartment. It was a warm summer day. I was about to start my second year of volleyball at Kirkwood Community College. I had not heard much from colleges, which was abnormal at this point, I thought.

That day, I stood out front waiting for a hand delivered a stack of bills I was now responsible for. I am sure most people my age had taken responsibility for this but I was looking at something I had never seen before. I had no idea how to do this or how I was going to do this. There I was in a sweaty shock, standing outside alone, out of breath.

I can count on one hand the number of times the world stood still around me and everything went silent. This was one of those moments. It was as if the whole entire world I had known before then was crumbling down around me. How was I supposed to do this? I would have to work or something. I would have to get serious about my life.

For the first time in my life I decided maybe it was time to give up this dream I had been working so hard for. This broke a piece of me more than I realized at that point. Right there, I gave it all up. The world freezing around me, I decided I better start getting serious. Dream a lot more realistically. I had a meeting with my coach Jill Williams shortly after being handed those bills. My mind was spinning away and she pulled me back in.

When my entire world was crumbling in front of me, she was there to remind me. We should all hope to have a person there ready and waiting to help in these moments. Coaches have always been that for me. When I was done letting Jill into my manic and insecure mind, she changed my life. She reminded me how capable I was of handling this. I sort of looked around as if she was talking to some adult that just couldn't be me.

Could I really handle this? Was this a doable assignment for me? I'd kind of had a constant back up in life. I always had someone there to guide me to a home unit to find security and self in.

That day, it became just me as it was always meant to be. The day my dream died, I was nineteen. I said no to my childish unrealistic dreams of pursuing athletics as an option. I gave up and decided that it was over without a second thought. I don't remember crying, but I'm sure I did. I had wanted this since I was thirteen and a stack of bills was a big enough blow to have me wanting to give up everything I had longed for.

After my meeting with coach, I knew that my dreams were absolutely over. Like the athlete I was, I knew I had to create a new, more realistic vision for my life. The only one I had ever planned on had just came to a screeching hault. It was like dreaming 30 feet below ground. I was hurt and dreaming up the plan for the rest of my life. That is why we need time for dream deaths. We shouldn't make decisions here, we're too hurt. Dreamers need time to recover. I needed time to find my way out of this darkness to dream again, but I never did.

I decided that division one athlete was plan A and I was no longer deserving of that life. So, I started figuring out plan B. That plan looked like a scaled down version of what I was willing to accept I deserved. I got serious about school more than sports for the first time in life. I was finally experiencing what everyone talked about in my hometown. People had told me to scale it down. People had told me this would have to end. People had told me to be realistic. But I dreamt big anyways.

My whole heart hurt planning out this lesser version. But it was what had to happen. I had failed to live up to the bigness of my life. It was time to give up. The new plan sounded like a lot less.

People's comments added to this low point in my life and it was all done. I felt stupid. Lost. Hopeless. I hadn't ever planned on that dream coming to an end even though so many people had told me I should. I believed. There was no helping me out of this moment. My coach gave me what I needed to hear. "You can do this. You are capable. Do this the way you want. Welcome to life."

People apart from her were not so inspiring. Everyone else seemed to laugh and were rather unsurprised that I had come to this place. Well Hanna, time to pick something else. No more volleyball. I started working more to pay bills like a real adult. That moment I declared a new major, a more focused adult-like major. There was a part of me that still thought I could make an unrealistic dream happen. So, I attempted art as a career and picked graphic design as a major. That led to more comments, opinions, and disbelief about my ability to make intelligent dreams and decisions.

Avoidance

Every part of me wanted to avoid everyone I had ever known. Remember the part where I wanted to be that hometown hero? The thing about that is when that's the goal and you fall short, you don't go back. From that point on, I acted as if I knew no one. Unfortunately, the internet existed by then and there was no shadow I could stay hidden behind.

People knew I didn't make it. It really didn't matter. They knew I was going to fall short the second I signed, but no one said it to my face. They did what good Iowans do. Passive aggressively attack me with questions about my path. About the time that I gave up on my dream, those comments flooded back in like a river running through my mind. "WHAT is your major?" "Really...just volleyball? You realize you have to go to school too, right?" "You can't major in volleyball." "What's the plan after that ends?"

How dumb. How ill prepared for life I was. I felt the size of an ant. I couldn't go back home and face everyone who told me to plan on this end. I couldn't go back and let everyone know I failed. I couldn't go back and let people see a kid with a broken heart, dreamless and hopeless. I avoided everyone. I was hoping they would forget all of that audacious talk about my volleyball dreams, but they didn't. I just wanted so bad to make my town proud and I had done the exact opposite.

When I started my podcast, I focused on that moment as where my life went wrong. After a couple of months discussing my dreams, I would realize that moment was far from it. Remember the doctor dream? Well at some point, I was led to look at that too. The fog that existed around that had removed it from my brain as significant, but when I revisited it I found less fog and more memory.

Less Fog

"Hanna, if you want to be a doctor you will have to have a lot of money and be very good at math," said a teacher I still can't place today.

That day a piece of me forever faded. That was the moment I gave away my say. It seems so unimportant and small. So silly, and at seven, a little dramatic. I can't remember the teacher because the entire memory is still a little blurry. But I can see my tin-foil stethoscope my mom made me fiddling through my fingers as the teacher addressed me. I can feel my face flush with embarrassment the moment I realize I got it wrong. I can feel my entire body and heart shrink all at once.

I got career day wrong. I couldn't even get that right. I knew I had gotten it wrong because as I sat there, I quickly remembered how my entire life up to that point had revolved around uncomfortable conversations about money. Enough that I had at least gathered enough proof leading up to that moment to know that the need of a lot of money and me did not mix.

I was also very aware of my less-than-average brain which teetered somewhere around smart enough to fit in. As I sat there twiddling foil, I could feel my doctor dream die inside of me. I brought this moment to life on my podcast and it was as if I was there again in real-time. They both felt the exact same. The sinking. The shrinking. I knew it was too good to be true. When the teacher said come dressed as what you want to be when you grow up, I now knew for some kids that meant anything and for kids like me it was conditional. It hadn't been spoken so clearly to me before this moment. It was likely the first time I had put it all together and it was definitely the last time I was going to be caught looking dumb again. I'm not smart enough to make this decision. I am not privileged or wealthy enough to believe I could climb a ladder that tall. I will wait. Kids like me just have to wait for someone to come along and tap them on the shoulder, so wait I did.

Not being smart followed me around for longer than I would like to admit. My brain just worked in ways that were different from most. The hum of all things required my utmost attention and that usually left me looking dumb and distracted. My mind was always ever-flowing. Constantly spinning from one direction to the next. It felt best in environments that were expansive and longing for vision. Brains like mine didn't have many seats where it was welcomed with open arms.

A school desk. No. A quiet dinner table. No. An assignment. No. When I could hone in on a hum, expansive discovery always followed. You couldn't find a kid more engaged than me, but finding a hum worth digging into that was big but small at the same time that took constant redirection. That took constant work by someone to pull me and my wandering mind back in.

At most basic descriptions, people would call my mind's rhythm bizarre, but I have come to know it as beautiful in the right context. I would find much later in life that I am quite intelligent. The way my mind works is one of wonder. It didn't fit in school because school was not made to fit minds like mine.

I couldn't help but be all over the place. I lived in a world too expansive and filled with things to wonder about. So I was smart after all. Where I was trying to fit was the problem. There was no mold for me and how I operated. Later in life I would discover maybe I was born to break it.

The teacher is not meant to be presented as a villain in this story. That teacher is a mere data point in my existence. That teacher was likely projecting a story told to them once about their own dreams. That one storyline threw an exponential twist in my life story, but it's not that person's fault. Usually those that love us project and protect in this same way. When they said I wasn't smart enough, that was easily applied to my beliefs about my worth, but the real impact was the overwhelming fact that I had gotten the choice wrong. So, the interpretation of that which broadened the impact was that I wasn't allowed to decide what my life should look like.

Not getting career day right sent me spiraling into a lifetime of decisions made for me. If I was not living a life privileged enough to make my own choices, I should look to those who are to make them for me. I like to think that my dream of being an athlete was my choice, but upon further examination that too was just me waiting for someone to tell me where to go next.

After I was told that my doctor dream didn't fit someone like me, my shiny bright self just thought optimistically this is how life works. The chosen ones choose for themselves AND then choose for people like me. Perfect.

Here's how that panned out

There I stood at seven, waiting for a decision to come down. Waiting for someone to choose me as specially gifted and worth noting. Since I was tall at an early age, by third grade the world had told me what to be. Luckily, I didn't have to wait long because I have come to learn a dreamless Hanna is not meant to live in this world. I spent a few years in between just waiting and then I decided upon the most repetitive comment from the outside world. I would be a basketball player. When people saw me towering over most kids my age would respond with, "My you are tall, I hope you play basketball." It never failed. I am sure any slightly above-average tall person has this same memory of the world interpreting their height as an obvious skill set extension to basketball.

For most, it was probably annoying. For me, it was confirmation. That was all I needed. I latched on to that "assigned" dream like a moth to a flame. Basketball was it the world had decided. I did not take this assignment lightly as I felt so excited to have already been chosen so early after getting it wrong. I remember feeling like I was one of the blessed purpose filled humans that got to live their dream their whole life. Obsession had clearly set in. Direction established. Life aligned. Basketball posters filled my room and practice and tournament schedules filled my days. I spent most nights shooting hoops in the driveway with my little brother and neighborhood kids. Basketball was the dream, the newly assigned direction. It was my focused hum.

That dream got a couple of upgrades along the way. People had told me it must be basketball, but upon entering the volleyball scene, I found an even more open and accepting audience, so I moved there. The basketball dream was assigned by others and so was volleyball. Luckily I had a coach that made it a point to convince me this could be an assigned path too. It didn't take much to move the dream over. Varsity jerseys, fanatic crowds, and an undeniable skill set for the sport made it an acceptable move.

Where to next

The next move was a harder assignment. After my dream died, I had to dream of a life much more stable and a lot less satisfying, but society's assigned dream being rejected left me questioning my ability to dream altogether. So I sat waiting again for someone to give me my next life assignment. I made a couple attempts to decide, only to come to the same conclusion...that I was not privileged or intelligent enough to decide. It seems insane right, that someone would just wait on the world to decide their life, but knives cut deep and the one cut into me unknowingly that fateful career day had left a wound that took decades to heal.

After the moment I realized I wasn't achieving a career in sports, I wandered for a couple of months like a lost puppy. Are you my dream? Are you my dream? I would wonder and wind each college course and semester.

Then one day it happened. I had chosen a career in graphic design kind of out of spite. I still wanted to rebel against societal norms and show the world that I could just do what I wanted, but most of me was still that lost puppy waiting to be shown acceptance and next steps.

Graphic design classes were fine. I struggled to hone in and obsess over the significance of one line being a degree on or off making a difference, but it did, and my lack of empathy for the lines was glaring.

My teacher noticed this lack of skill set right away. I did fine in class and had amazing concepts but lacked creative follow-through of concepts for accurate and creative delivery. I was angry at myself because it was becoming evident that I would soon be standing with a teacher who would be forced to deliver the news that Hanna had gotten career day wrong yet again, and deliver he did.

It was the best day I had in my entire college career. Most people probably would have seen this day as the ending of a passion. I saw it as the perfect redirection. My professor lovingly told me that concept and interactions were a rarity with my skill set and that a career in marketing, selling, and directing design might be a better fit.

I enrolled in that college course career path the next day. I would spend my next two years continuing to play and obsess over volleyball but making my way towards a professional degree in public relations and marketing.

The new plan: work in public relations at a hospital (I came up with it that day). The additional plan: be a high school volleyball coach. That was it for life. Forever.

This Path

Look at this path. Initial dream death at age seven followed with a season of lost and looking. Societal assignment of sports at age ten. Deep dive into the possibilities. Dream, obsess, work. Dream death of athletic career at age nineteen followed with another season of lost and looking. Attempt to self-assign graphic design. Dream, obsess, work. Only to be shown once again that I was not good enough to just decide. Dream death at age nineteen of my creative career. Professor assignment of marketing. Deep dive into possibilities. Dream, obsess, work. That is where that ended.

I took that assignment and created an entire life around it. There were pieces I wasn't willing to let go and there were dreams I created on my own, but it all revolved around what society would hand me as an assignment for my life. I dreamt fearlessly with those assigned dreams. They felt comfortable and secure compared to my own, which felt nauseating and impossible. These were the stories. I couldn't let go of an identity society told me was me. It felt wrong to look outside of what society assigned as acceptable for my life.

I set what felt like crazy goals. To work in public relations at a hospital (remember the whisper to change lives?) Healthcare felt like a worthy life-changing cause. Actually, my professor moment lined up perfectly with the first time I watched the Denzel Washington movie John Q. In that movie, there was an administrator who was made out to be heartless. I knew my degree likely didn't line up with an admin but I figured public relations would somehow put me close enough. I could be the caring, loving, and kind administrator who changed people's lives with my light and love for people and the work. It seemed like an aligned calling. A divine path. I was good at interesting assignments and marketing them to alignment. Might have been the degree, might have just been me.

The other dream was to be a head high school volleyball coach. I wasn't too scared to release my athlete identity. I felt like I had more to prove in athletics like my time was not up and that I wasn't wrong that I belonged on big stages in this sport. I was planning to show the world that what they knew of me as an athlete was wrong.

I was not a failure. I was destined for more. Plus, I just wasn't all that sure of myself as a working professional, so it felt good to keep something I was sure of during the first identity crisis moments of my adult years.

Big Stages

One of the dreams I didn't cover that I set alongside the goal of being a division one basketball athlete was to win a state title. All of this alignment happened what seems like all at once looking back. That winter, our girls' high school basketball team had made it to the state basketball tournament. Our school did this amazing thing where the teams that made it to state parade around school with a pep band getting signs, send offs, and high fives from all of the younger students. It was quite aspirational.

I got a high five from the only female division athlete I ever knew existed. Sarah Hippen. I knew I wanted to be just like her. Tall, college recruited, and on the way to win a state title. I bought a necklace at the state basketball tournament. The day I put it on, I promised myself I would one day win a state title. That summer, I bet my dad I would be a division one college athlete.

When I was searching for a new identity while still clinging to the old, I remembered one of those goals could still serve as a proof point to my hometown that I was still capable of coming back with the trophy. I was twenty-two and I was about to marry the love of my life. I had new goals and was actively figuring who the world wanted me to be with this newly adopted plan B.

I had spent five years stumbling from job to job telling myself it fit when the perfect opportunities arrived hand in hand. By the age of twenty-seven I had accomplished everything I set as goals from that broken dream place. I moved pretty close to my hometown, settled down, and started a life. House, kids, husband, and a shiny SUV. I had gotten a job at a local hospital in public relations and I had taken over as a head coach of a high school volleyball team not far from the hospital I worked at.

So what does one do from there? I figured this is when people start climbing or maybe this is where dreams fade from importance and kids take over. I thought that might be a good option, maybe I had the spotlight long enough. My only problem with that was the type of environment I was raised in…Always speaking words to offer up big dreams being an option but never action that matched. No stories that could convince me of what was possible. So, while I had heard my dreams were valid and important at home, I didn't see any action that followed that closely.

That may be one of my pet peeves in life…words not matching action. Either way, the choice was mine. Remain in pursuit of a life I love or slowly fade from existence. Since I was not willing to drop my significance in life for my children's sake and sanity, I decided I should start climbing instead. No real reason except I was going to be bored if I didn't and I didn't want my kids to not chase their dreams.

I was back to waiting again. Waiting for the world to see me. Waiting for someone to show up and pick me. It didn't take long in either environment. By my twenty-seventh birthday, I had stumbled my way to my first state tournament appearance in my inaugural season as a head coach. I was working to gain respect in my position at the hospital as a valued team member who could help with system expansion and strategic leadership. I was not fading in life. I was finding heightened success faster than I ever thought. Climb. Climb. Climb. I found a faster pace than I had ever operated in managing two kids under four, a full-time job, along with a self-induced year-round coaching job.

The success was an ultimate high for me. There was always more to get. Always more trophies, more awards, and more positions. My second year of coaching, we played for a state title and we ended up runners up. I became obsessed like never before. I was out to prove myself and how I belonged here. To prove I was worthy of space with this sport. I was gaining more titles and seats at tables in my day job. I moved from one service line to the entire hospital and the high was addicting. I was high performing and delivering all day every day. So long as everything stayed in perfect unison I could keep operating at the hum. I had not an ounce of time to myself. Every second outside of work was spent barely sleeping and mostly preparing for the race coming up that would be the next day.

It was great. I showed up and served everyone. Everyone but the people I actually cared about. When I would stumble home from the hum of the day where there were obvious ways to win, I would fade away. I had poured out everything I had everyday. So home was getting what was left of a fading power pack. Just drips, but what was the worth in saving to serve my home? To me, there were no awards for top parent, or best wife, so with the beliefs I had adopted why would they get my time. It wasn't a paid position. It would not go on my resume. So barely enough just had to be enough.

I showed up late to everything. I was nowhere in my life. I was a mere body at events where my mind constantly worked to escape. I wanted to be where I was comfortable performing, working for worth, and delivering new ways to win. I was losing everyone I loved most. Luckily my kids just knew this as mom. I was fun for about two seconds a day, but they mostly served as another thing I could say I managed in a day. Just another impressive stat to take into account when the decision makers looked at my resume. And she has two young kids.

Now don't get me wrong, kids were the most wonderful and terrible decision I ever made and continue making every day. Wonderful in how they build you like nothing else can and terrible because there is no way to have ever known if you won. It terrifies me to this day. My friend Beth says the measure is a good human, and I have adopted that as mine as well. Either way, my babies and husband only knew a percentage of the human I was. To be honest, that was all I had come to believe that was all they needed as well.

Shocked

At twenty-nine, I stood in disbelief, my entire body shocked still. People rushed all around me, noise erupted, and a moment I had played in my mind so many times was here. My athletes piled on one another on the court, my coaching staff stood as shocked in the moment as I was, and shortly after the shock faded, there I was holding a 3A Iowa Volleyball State Championship trophy in my hands. I remember looking up at the crowd trying to process this dream come true. A moment later, the realization set in that I have more than I could have ever dreamt in this space and in my life. This was as good as it was going to get. It all set in. An inescapable realization that this wasn't "it" either was spiraling in my head. I was somewhere between nirvana and psychosis which is the most interesting place I have ever been mentally.

Shortly after the tournament, the red carpets I had longed for were rolled out. I sat at tables with people I had grown up idolizing. They valued my opinions and mindset when it came to the game. I floated above my realization for a while after. My new job became convincing myself this fit because I had finally found acceptance in a game where rejection had become my calling card. I wanted it to fit. I wanted to belong. I didn't want to keep floating and not fitting. Intuition was screaming at this point. Even though it was wrong, it was at least the comfortable kind. I figured if I just kept climbing, a higher paycheck, nicer car, bigger house, status level, or accomplishment could cover my bubbling inaptitude for life.

I was selected for things I didn't deserve during this sprint season of my life. From the age of twenty-seven to thirty, I was only capable of keeping everyone's heads above water but I had everything and more than I had ever asked for. Trophy in hand, crowds screaming. I would realize the sprint had to stop for my life to start. If this wasn't it, what was?

I'm thankful for the love shown to me during this season. People gave me grace I did not deserve. I served everyone and no one that mattered for those four years. The goal was to get picked, but when I did, I realized it was just the beginning of another dream death. It was yet another moment to go to work to figure out what I got wrong with my career day selection this time. I knew at thirty I could no longer keep up the pace. My lack of presence stole my soul and I wanted desperately to start showing up as a whole person in my life.

The death of one dream and moving to the next isn't the story ending moment that I experienced when we sit with the reality that it is meant to keep us moving forward. I believe my success in that sprint season was pushing a pace that would eventually slow me to this realization. I also believe I was given a fast pass to quicken my arrival to this moment. The world is spinning in the direction of our upward arrival if we choose it.

The second that state title dream came true, it all set it. This was everything I had ever wanted. my life was officially done. Or was it?

I knew this time this was not something worth sprinting past again. It was not something I would let someone decide for me again. This dream death would not set me up for less than. I wanted a chance to dream from a place of truth to me instead of society.

Dark Spot

So what's with all the drumming up of bad memories? Why recall ALL the dream death?

Well, it forces surrender, and for me it proved to necessary for this to work.

When I started thinking about my dreams, it was always easy to find it sunny. Optimism is my default, which most people would generally categorize as the best trait to have in life. It is and is not.

Even though I had lived an awesome life, I had come to a wall. The problem with the wall was I had colored it yellow. My optimism could not see it as what it was. A wall standing in front of me.

To me, it was just another opportunity to cover it up with some fun posters and call it a day. I could always make it brighter. I could always find the opportunity. If I had never posed my dream in this extreme of a way, I would have never fully recognized it for what it was. A death. A dark spot. An ending.

My podcast art, although not intentionally, reflects this. It's a wall like most of us have come to. A wall that must be broken through. A wall that, even when painted yellow, is still a wall. It still has a need to be broken down and built back up again. Surrender offers that. It structures the extreme. It forces the discomfort. Discomfort for which we may blaze on by and begin to think we can outrun.

I will say here that we can't slow down enough for this part. Running only makes it worse. When I tried to outrun my whisper, it chased me down with a vengeance. It found me, and there was no optimism or motivation to save me from it. I hit what was rock bottom for me. I had lost all of my hope. I would offhandedly joke about taking my own life on a day-to-day basis.

Without dreams, I had nothing that spoke to me. Without direction, I had nowhere to go. I had lost all hope. The discovery of my dream death dropped me even lower. So, it would seem this is something I could have just covered up, and most will, but eventually it catches up no matter what. No matter how fast and full our lives are. No matter how much we do for the world. No matter who we pray to. It all catches up eventually.

I believe it's the energy dissonance. Our bodies and minds are pretty pro us. All the time. When we see something showing up as the opposite, I believe it's an attempt to force the surrender. The surrender to what we hear or what we know, that we're tired of fighting. Maybe that's a career, relationship, or long time quarrel we've held onto for far too long. Our bodies aren't built to attack themselves. My dream dissonance had left my body stewing against itself for far too long.

No diagnosis

I spent most of my childhood in and out of hospitals. It was never for anything related to one another, I just always had "something." Broken bones, sicknesses, strange conditions, and pretty much anything else that took an awkwardly long time to diagnose.

One of the constant recurring issues was digestion issues. This followed me my entire life starting at the age of seven. Now, since I had so many issues as a kid, I never thought much of it. This is just my body doing me wrong, I would think.

A term adopted by my family was, "Only Hanna," which is always related to weird and unrecognizable issues. But around the time I started on this work, I would start to see my first relief of the digestion issues I was told would follow me like a dark cloud for life.

At seven, my dream died and I started silencing the human I was meant to be. I started showing up to fit a box of existence that was never meant for me.

That year, I would start to develop horrible stomach aches and pain. Doctors could not figure it out. About six months into testing and appointments all to no avail, doctors would start to label me a kid that just wanted to miss school. Luckily, my mom is a no-holds-barred mama bear and she went to bat for me and the once happy, bubbly, not a care in the world kid I was before the pain.

Eventually, after a year and a half of tests, trials, medicines, and imagining that they decided to scope the area and see what nothing else seemed to show, they would find my appendix doubled in size and wrapped around my colon. Not inflamed, just weird and causing unexplainable pain. It was removed and all was fixed until it wasn't again.

Now looking back, I can see the patterns. That moment these digestive issues began, I was sinking into the person I believed I had to be. I was shrinking to fit what I was told I should be. I had just begun experimenting with trying to be someone I was not, and my body was actively rejecting it. My body was fighting for me. It was fighting for my truth. This would show up again at age nine with the same path to final diagnosis after a year and half in and out of hospitals all to no avail.

It would show up again at age twelve with no solution or diagnosis, just medicine for heartburn. It would worsen by age fifteen, which is when doctors would start the first discussion about this being a life issue that was just going to stick.

It would rear its ugly head in college, landing me in some emergency room visits with the same diagnosis of lifetime issues. Nothing we can do but keep you on daily laxatives and fiber meds. That eventually lent itself to a severe eating disorder at age twenty. I was sick of experiencing the world this way. It was hard to exist in a body that was so full and bloated all the time. At least when I was not eating and throwing up most meals, I wasn't bloated for the first time in forever. My body was fighting for me. Attempting to give me signals...Signals that I was running to the doctor to try to heal. They couldn't find anything because it started as just dissonance. My heart, soul, body, and mind all agree this wasn't right for me and they showed up to fight. To get people to take note, to maybe get me to pay attention.

I wouldn't know enough to know that this is what was happening, but now retracing the steps and noticing the patterns, it's easy to see.

Later in my work, I would discover chakras and start overlying that on my path. The solar plexus chakra controls our ability to be confident and in control of our lives. Both of which I felt I abandoned at seven on career day. Issues with the solar plexus can present as digestive issues like ulcers, heartburn, eating disorders, and indigestion, all of which I suffered with at different times since the age of seven. Solar plexus is chakra of our personal power. All of which I unquestionably owned until that fateful career day. Stomach issues that have completely gone away a year and half after taking back my power to live life on my terms.

THE SURRENDER

CHAPTER FOUR

Story Surrender

Prerequisite

This is why the surrender is so very important. It is not about bringing up the old to bring you down. It is about bringing it up so we can find where it all began. So we can trace patterns and overlay the new information we bring into the discovery. I know it sucks, and for an intrinsic optimist, believe me it was the hardest part. I really just wanted to hang some yellow posters and help people believe in themselves. Which I could have probably done, but I also knew the color of the wall didn't matter for me. So it had to look different. It would have to be a deeper path to discovery.

While I don't want any of us to re-experience the pain, we may find that we have to go there to know where to go next. It's our personal history application. It gives us the ability to know what needs to be brought along to this new season. Some things we will dust off and remember and pick them up. I had to go back to dust off and remember the bright bubbling being that was me before the world rocked her. I had to go back and drop the disbelief that I had copy pasted from that one experience at the age of seven.

Surrender isn't about digging up old scars as much as it is about remembering what was left there when it happened. Then we get to decide what we dust off and what we drop from those moments.

We should all recognize that our experiences are just ours. It will do us no good to compare our painful pasts to other people even though we'll want to. It will likely not do us any good to go back to these moments, find the people who hurt us, and try to get closure.

In some instances, that may be extremely important, but in most, it will leave us involving another person in work that is meant to just be about you. I hope that we don't allow ourselves to wrap someone else in this web, as it likely lessens the accountability of the surrender. There is nothing anyone can do for us on this self-discovery path. All paths lead back to us. All truths to our interpretation of the story.

This is the part where the work gets real. Real sucky. I had a long, long list of reasons why my dreams didn't come true. A long list of people who could take the fall as well. It couldn't have been me. But the truth is, none of that mattered. Who did what, how it impacted me, none of it mattered one bit. I was here. I was in the middle of a life I liked but wasn't satisfied with. I was in the middle of a perfectly imperfect life.

Since none of it was my fault, it was really easy to ride the easy train on this one. I could blame my body for giving up on me and not allowing me to continue my journey with sports. I could blame my income or lack of opportunity on my needing to move back home. I could blame my parents for not putting me in the right clubs to get recruited. I could blame my coaches for not pushing me hard enough and working to find me somewhere to follow my dreams. I could blame my kids for taking my money and time, therefore taking my ability to climb guilt free. I could blame schedules, my spouse, my boss, my job, or anything really.

It was quite easy to find scapegoats. It was never me and it never had to be. I could depend on my excuses and "why" and "why not" forever, and since those reasons were endless, so was resentment.

This anger... The truth was I felt more comfortable angry than I did happy at this point in my life. It was almost as if my angry self was the only reminder of the passion I used to have for things. Now it was gone except when I got mad. It didn't take much, and my anger fits were quite entertaining. I could spiral down entire rabbit holes for "why this" or "why that" and have an extremely convincing case to make. Most of the room would, at minimum, be entertained if not convinced to rally their own anger and join in. It gave me spotlights and made me feel fire. But it was never enough. Fire was always doused or over-thought when I returned home. A darkness was always sure to follow. I could blame anyone and anything and the darkness remained.

The blame didn't remove the pain, it just removed the responsibility. No matter how much I removed my responsibility, the pain of no dreams didn't fade. The pain of experiencing life in fits of passion instead of being weaved throughout hurt worse than anything I had experienced in life. There was never going to be one single thing to blame that ended the cycle. I had to start taking responsibility or at least owning the fact that my life was supposed to happen this way.

It's a Wonderful(ish) Life

This is not a hopeless romantic novel about life. I was furious at the wonderful life I had created myself. A lot of George Bailey vibes. I had big plans and then life just kept happening to me. But I didn't have a "dive in the ice to save an angel" moment. So I created mine.

I researched it and studied it and kept trying to find out what happiness was all about anyways. I could trick myself into being happy just fine. I could motivate myself for long periods of time, but I always came back underwhelmed about my life. I couldn't shake the fact that I wanted more than I was getting, but I couldn't even adequately explain what it was that I wanted. I just knew it wasn't what I had.

Before my conference, I had a moment that shook me almost as much as the snow day moment. In January, I'd had that blow up, which led me to the doctors, which led me to even more anger, which led me to another major milestone moment that forced the issue of me needing to fix my life.

I was getting ready for a wedding and I couldn't explain it, but I just felt mad. Majorly mad. Everyone in my house could feel my anger. It was as if it was boiling up in the entire house. I was putting on my makeup and curling my hair when it hit me: I won't ever have any exciting milestones like this ever again. I'm done having showers, weddings, showers, celebrations, babies... I'm done. My anger rose even more. My heart sank and tears started streaming down my face. It was all like an evil buildup, I thought. You're supposed to grow up and do all the things, but once you do, that's it. You're just done. Then it's just someone else's turn forever. FOREVERRRRR.

Come on...this couldn't be it. But it was. I got ready for the wedding and we left. Everything inside of me was still jumbled up and I felt dazed and confused. That night, I drank stupid amounts of alcohol. I just wanted to get this anger out. I just wanted to feel as fine as my life looked. Everything in me was wanting to come out, wishing it existed or mattered in this world, but I knew that night it didn't. So I drowned out all of the confusion.

It didn't help. It left me spinning, hungover, even more angry, and now embarrassed. It also did nothing to help process the feelings. But just like we started this section, I had to start owning some responsibility for this work. So I stopped drinking, shopping, and working excessively and started to get serious about changing my life. To get serious about finding happiness or at least experiencing it more than just on a spotlight occasion. The joy in my life did not need to depend on some major milestone. I had to find a way to do it without a crutch or quick fix option. I needed to experience the real me again. Happy-go-lucky and confident me.

Ditch the Blame

I had blamed my state, my ancestors, my upbringing, and pretty much everything for why I was unhappy. I had blamed my small-town upbringing for so long that about a month after that wedding blow up, we traveled to Oregon to see about settling some new roots. Maybe it was the soil, maybe it was the roots, but it definitely was just easier to point the finger and leave it all in the dust.

If I wasn't the one to blame, then I was still doing okay. On the trip to Oregon, we set out to prove two things to ourselves. We wanted to prove that Iowan's were not the only ones who were nice in this world and we wanted to prove that people could live other places.

We hadn't really known many people who did, so while that may not be important for most since it seems rather obvious, it wasn't that obvious to us. Oregon was even more amazing than promised. I mostly felt certain of my untimely death as we drove around and up and down the mountains, but other than that, it proved to be one of the most breathtaking places I had experienced to date. It was an amazing new promise. It was an amazing new plan. Oregon could save us. Iowa was the problem. Again, not me.

We came home and made exciting new plans to head out west. It would take us approximately two years to save enough of a nest egg to head that way without jobs secured prior. Then we just went to work. That really was the plan. Our lives in Iowa could never and would never be enough. So we had started planning our exit.

We figured it would be easier to leave before the kids got comfortable and before we got even more comfortable. Two years seemed like enough of a window to set a plan to exist elsewhere. To be happy later and to hate every second in between. Iowa had done us wrong in more ways than one, and so we thought leaving there had to be the answer. If our lives were meant to be bigger, then maybe Iowa couldn't be the place for that to happen. We could blame everyone for where our feet were still planted, but we had at least finally taken accountability for the fact that we could change that.

When we got back, the accountability set in. If we wanted to change our lives, we were the only ones who could make it happen. I would sit crunching numbers and researching jobs. My husband would sit looking at housing, schools, and daycares. This was important because it was the first time we took part in the change we wanted in our lives. This was a whole chapter advance from where we had been in our lives just letting it all happen to us. This was a moment that was set in stone that if we wanted to go, it was in our control. If we stayed, that was as well.

Iowa didn't just happen to us by not making a different choice but complaining we were still making an active choice to stay. Not finding a way out of anger is an amazing way to stay exactly where we are. I fought my smallness most of my life. I wished I was from anywhere bigger...anywhere, but never was. Again, none of this was the problem. I never accepted my accountability for all of this at all. I had skipped the portion where I made the decisions that had built the life I wasn't excited about. Whether I wanted to acknowledge it or not, I was responsible for all of this. For Iowa, for the lack of presence, and for the anger. I was the angriest optimist to ever exist.

The wedding and the trip pushed my buttons and sat me up in my own life for the first time ever. They weren't breaking points as much as they were mile markers. They were "take note" moments leading up to a big breakthrough. These moments had started the wave of realization, a wave without which may have never brought me to my breaking point, may have never sent me to my knees, the realization that I had everything I needed to change my life.

If I wanted to move to Oregon, I could. If I wanted to live my dreams, I could. If I wanted to be happy, I could. I could make it all happen if I would just decide that this is how it was all meant to happen. Those ripples led to the big wave in my life. They sent out shock waves to get parts of me to pay attention. Parts I had turned off long ago.

This journey is not one where the switch just flips over forever. It's a continued pursuit. It happens in ripples that lead to waves. So don't watch only for waves. Look for what doesn't work out and look for where nothing seems to be. That might just be the moment that ripples the changes into existence. Those two ripples moved me from anger to accountability, not in one fell swoop, but in more and more adoption over time. I was angry and then I surrendered because what was could never not be. It was always me and I could run...I could move...I could attempt to change who I became, but that part would always be there whether I ran or surrendered. The attempt to move was another crutch to hold onto for why it all went wrong. It would have sent us spiraling for happiness we couldn't have found even climbing the tallest mountain. Should we just surrender the notion that what ripples is in our control and go on with our lives oblivious, but searching to sow it all together.

CHAPTER FIVE

Examination

This is me

What led to this moment is exactly what was meant to happen. Even if it wasn't, what can I do about any of that now? It took coming back to that fact over and over for a little while, because of how anger and resentment had become second nature.

For me, that meant choosing presence instead of looking too far into the future and ignoring what is or living in anger over what was. I kept bouncing back and forth. Always living too far forward to enjoy what was or too far back trying to protect what wasn't. My mind was in a race that only I was in. Overthinking about every interaction trying to pin every word to a storyline I was longing to forget. The process of examination is the hardest part. It took facing a lot of things I had never come to terms with. It took allowing accountability for things I was not entirely responsible for, but found myself plagued with as a storyline. How each person navigates this is personal and important to intuitively follow your own path.

While it is good to utilize information from others, it will also be vital to work and get in touch with your inner knowing. The voice as it will. When we let go of others' guidance, we can begin to find our way back to our own. As we do that, we can begin to engage a louder voice. The undoing of beliefs is about choosing something new. It is officially time to begin looking at what we keep and what we leave behind.

Some things are not meant to stay in your storyline. I had parts of my story that were painful non-truths upon examination. So

I had to work to write something new. I had to sit in the truth of that pain to find a way to a new belief that I wanted so badly to believe I deserved.

When I dropped some things, I realized how much space freed up as a result. Although, some things I expected to drop out didn't and most did and I could walk in a lighter, more lovely existence. The untruths we find in this moment will serve as guides for the comeback to self-love. We have spent too many years infecting our natural light vibration with this venom. It's time to give it up. It's time to find what deserves to stay and what has to go when it comes to you and what we know to be true. Some things are meant to stay and others are meant to end.

Over time, I got more open about that examination. Every door shall come to question in this stage. Dreams are a great place to start because of how we learned to navigate life with or without them. They come with a lot of disbelief if taught wrong from an early age. The greatest thing I did was stay open in the examination of my truths, values, and guiding principles. It's okay I allowed myself to push back on things I never expected to push back on. It was important to see what held in this moment of time. I found things meant to stay didn't crumble under pressure. This is the time to see what stands up and what holds on.

I like to think of this as the tornado portion of the ride. This time with a controlled spin only examining when we have made room to look at the next truth to undo. I was attempting to tear the house I had built my life on back down to the studs or maybe even the foundation. I found it wasn't all that helpful to keep building on a house with an unsteady foundation.

It felt like I was ripping apart everything I had come to know.

I had clung onto this version for too long finding only comfort and no growth. I found this version of myself couldn't survive this new path. The vibrations are too differing to see both thrive. I had to leave one at the station.

I chose this path, while I wasn't perfect, over time I saw a bigger distance from who I was and who I knew I could be. Things that stuck and didn't serve were ripped off like wallpaper. It wasn't fun getting it started and some will stick around until I came back with the heavy remover, but once I got it going, the evidence of change proved more positive than the pain.

The truths that come down (I call them truths, which is what we have come to know them as) are often masquerading as lies with a fictitious name. We should not feel bad when we release what wasn't ours to hold onto.

We should love those who taught us their truths with hope that they might someday be our own. We should forgive ourselves for examining what is ours to keep even if it means letting go of something that was understood as utmost important to someone we love. This is our life, and while we're eternally grateful for all of the people who have loved us into existence, they were never meant to guide every part.

Most of what will be is up to us should we take responsibility back. These truths will fall, and along with it, pieces of your life might too. I know for me religion took a long examination. It was a truth that was given to me at birth, passed down from generation to generation, upon my careful examination, some things stuck but some didn't. This meant a major falling out with some people I really loved who couldn't understand the examination and the questioning of this normalized truth, but for me this was a big part of my shaky existence. So I had to let it go and I had to let people keep their truths as a part of their sacred wholeness just as I was examining and rebuilding mine.

This is hard in the examination phase. There are parts of us that want to sound the alarms and pull the blinders off those we know, but I caution against these conversations, as we never really know when people are open to examination. The very act of preaching to someone closed off to examination is a waste of time and energy. So keep it within when you can and share when asked. Since we will be in this season of examination for a while, we don't want to get everyone riled up and ready to fight us when we're already fragile as it is.

The world of safety, security, and comfort I had known was crumbling all around me. There's no need to help what already is and I find conversations around the truths you are uncovering in your life aren't usually all that helpful in movement anyways. People have to be ready, and when they are, I find they generally ask. But collecting a group of followers with every truth you uncover will likely leave us exhausted of reserves we will need to make it through this season. It's okay to let people get there themselves because your focus is you getting there, not the rest of the world.

The deconstruction of things I once believed was a heavy process. Meticulously, I picked at what had been. Curiously, we push back against things we were taught as known truths. So as you break these things down, there is needed recovery. It is like a death and it very much is. There will be a rebirth, a moment where your shiny new self shows up in this world like it never has before. This can only happen following a severe upheaval.

As I deconstructed, I found things I still wanted, but I wanted them in different ways. I found an old tried and true chimney that I could build my new foundation around. There is so much room for reinvention here. The foundation has become a blank slate. The foundation now backed with verifiable truths in this life. Truths that I built around a life I felt excited to wake up and start living.

New Beliefs

Over time, I found what fit in this new belief space. I brought some old things back in and tried them on to see if they now fit where I wasn't sure they would. I teach classes on minimalism, and the application of those teachings helps a lot here. It was okay for some values to be packed up and stored in the basement for a while. I flushed out what I actually needed, wanted, and loved. Not all things that came into question were true or false, keep or throw. Some things will need to be stored. There was a chance that everything I was becoming would lead me right back where I was all along.

If that happens I will be happy to find that box still full of what it is and downstairs all packed up and ready. I do this with items in rooms. Until we know we can do without seventeen spatulas, maybe we just pack up ten of them. Maybe we find ten is not enough and we bring back all seventeen because we cook a lot and hate dishes or always need at least four per day. But maybe we realize seven is even too many, and over time as we whittle down what works, we find less need for more. We find more time for ourselves. I had spent time finding what truths stick and what I actually needed versus what I just wanted for comfort.

Self-Love

This new foundation should be built with intention. This process teaches things I never thought to ask. It questioned truths I would have never pushed back on. Through that, I discovered a stable foundation, one that is solid and true. A foundation worth building the rest of my life on.

Here is the one truth that has to be built in. I usually prompt, versus instruct, as I trust you as the source for everything that is. But this one I can't let go of. This is worth building the entire house around, and as cliche as it sounds, it's the single most important truth in all of this work. This is the chimney that must be built brick by brick. Self-love.

My old self is cringing as I write those words. I spent a lot of time making fun of people who had the time to practice the art of self-love. I would prop myself and my ego up on many jokes about the audacity of people with such time on their hands... Now this is more than just bath bombs, scented lotions, and the occasional spa day. This is love in its highest form. This is practicing an unrelenting belief of how amazing and deserving of love you are. This is deeper than just taking care of yourself, even though that is a great place to start.

The truth is, I hated those people who had time, not because they had something I would have never had (even though it was that too) but because they loved themselves enough to give time to them. They loved themselves enough to know what they even enjoyed.

This always perked my angry little head right up. So I would join in the making fun of anyone who had enough time to shower, bathe, read, write, sing, dance, or draw. To know yourself is to love yourself. I had spent most of my life hating everything I had ever been, so rewarding my mediocrity seemed pointless.

I wasn't raised in obvious hate. It was understated as a steady passive aggressive. Mostly, it was an undertone that I easily picked up on. It was in little spiteful comments. It was in conversations after the conversations. It was in whispers behind backs. While hate was never on display in public, it lined all the walls. It poisoned my ability to understand how to love myself. I was unaffected for a short time and then I adopted self-hate as the norm. I assumed everyone just hated themselves and secretly most of the people they surround themselves with as well, it seemed to me, their entire life.

This was a foundation that took a while to break as I didn't have much proof of the opposite being true. I definitely didn't have shining examples knocking down my door to mentor me either. Self-hate takes time to undo. For a lot of us, it can be etched into more than we would ever recognize. I didn't ever think self-love and dreams had anything to do with one another, but I would come to find it as a foundational principle of all dream work.

I was raised in a self-love desert. Most people around me had settled and were spitefully spinning into oblivion. So learning self-love took time. It wasn't that I couldn't apply it effectively as much as I didn't believe I was worthy of it. There was no monetary return in this practice that I could see directly, so why spend time there?

Not only that, I had been coached and taught in "normal" environments where there was no worth in blowing sunshine up people's a**es. So I had a lot of things to deconstruct around this. It seemed to be my strongest standing untruth that I would come to uncover.

This is the part where I am going to tell you to start blowing the sunshine up every orifice possible. Pardon my language here but I find the terminology absolutely endearing. The way to shift a belief is to look for proof of what you want to believe, so we have to shift from looking for proof of how terrible we are, to proof of how amazing or great we are. This is enough to start the shift. This is enough to change the vibration. It will be uncomfortable because self-love and feeling great about our lives is not normal, but the world needs something new. It needs the light we were meant to be. When we're given light, we can grow. So start blowing the sunshine.

Greatness Grounding

It was 2017. The volleyball team I was the head coach of started training for the season ahead of us. The season before, we had ended one game short of the school's first ever state title. We had come up with second place in the class 3A state finals.

I was starting my third season as head coach with a vengeance for how we had come up short. I'd spent nights, weekends, and mornings there almost every day since the ball dropped last season, planning a new approach and a way to come away with the title this season. At the beginning of that year, I polled the team, freshman through seniors. I asked them to list the top five volleyball programs in the state. 81% of the student athletes in my program didn't list us as one of the top programs. I am certain the other 19% had figured they should list us for a reason that was not explained or they actually believed it. Either way, 19% was not enough belief for me.

We spent the morning running the difference. I had no idea how to fix this. I am sure this is something that most coaches struggle with, so I was no different, but I knew when we came up short last year that it wasn't that we weren't good enough, it was that we didn't believe we were good enough.

Here that factoid was in plain statistics. 81%. That was the number I needed to shift. I found so many good resources on the internet for drills and team building, yet nothing that could shift a belief of not being good enough. Nothing that could help my team see themselves as worthy of playing in a title game and then worthy of winning it.

I was lost and frustrated. Then one day, I opened up a book, a book that I had wanted to read and bought even though I knew nothing about my schedule would open up an opportunity to allow me to dive in. So I did what I always did and opened up the first couple of chapters. I would get really motivated to read once in a while and pretend my way through a chapter or two. This was one of those times. I sat pretending and found a fact that didn't sit right with me. I closed the book and pondered it. I went to the internet and found even more alarming discoveries. Sheryl Sandberg stood on a stage and voiced that she didn't know what to do about it, but she was concerned. As was I, but I sat there thinking that doing nothing was more of an injustice. So I drafted an email to my coaching staff of 7th-12th grade that read:

I recently read a chapter in one of my books titled Lean In by Sheryl Sandberg. She talked about how females are turned down for next level jobs because they don't speak confidently about their accomplishments compared to their male counterparts. When I watched her TEDtalk on the topic, she said she didn't know what to do, and I don't either, but we had a group of athletes who should be practicing, owning their accomplishments, and speaking to them so they are ready when called on. So here is what I decided we are going to do: each day we will spend five to ten minutes having each athlete on each team individually speak to one great thing they accomplished that day. The only rules are that they must account for ownership of the accomplishment. They cannot pass it off to a team. Maybe it won't make a difference, but at least we can stand up and say we knew this and this is what we did.

Most of the next moments were met with eye rolling when I laid the plan out to my group of "way too cool" varsity kids. They showed up and did it anyways, and amazingly this became the best part of the day. Athletes would run in with their great things. It was as if we were doing something totally foreign. Celebrating accomplishments they felt good about each day.

That year, something significant shifted. While I didn't line this all the way up at the time, this was the answer to how a coach can shift 81% of players in the program not believing they were a top team. A coach couldn't do it with one big showing of significance. It took individual accomplishments, usually unrelated, to tap into the bigger, more significant accomplishments.

That year, we brought home the first state title the school had ever won. We actually brought home the first in the town of Waterloo, Iowa. It wasn't in the big belief of greatness; it was in the little steps of believing in ourselves along the way.

The consistency of showing up for ourselves and our greatness paid off big time. It created an environment of trust, truth, and authenticity I could have never intentionally created on my own. It also got female athletes talking confidently everyday about the things they were doing and owning them the whole way. We showed up as a different group of athletes that year. We became fierce supporters of the epicness' we saw exhibited in one another each day gathering around our greatness. Grounding our truth in how amazing we were in our everyday lives. It was four years before I started this work, but I find myself still in shock of the needles that moved that year. All because I was obsessed with solving a problem and winning a state title. One had nothing to do with the other, or so I thought. Yet here I am now, knowing they couldn't have been one without the other.

This story exhibits the root of the lack of belief. This team had grown up knowing they were good and saw glimmers, but never had consistent feedback of greatness related to volleyball. In our area, there are a couple of teams that have ruled the roost, rightfully so, for a very long time, so it was them and everyone else. We were a team of everyone else's, including and most notably, me. But that greatness grounding seemed to be enough to set a new stage. To believe we were more than we knew ourselves to be.

Work to find the root of where these lie is very important. This is usually related to lack. Things we constantly, sometimes unknowingly, fill our heads with. Once we discover where they came from, we can search for the proper solutions. If along the way you find that confidence is something you struggle with, greatness grounding might be an awesome practice for you. If you discover that you have major imposter syndrome, find some YouTube videos or some books that offer specific solutions for that.

More than anything, find where that voice is coming from so it can be shut down. This is all a personal mission. What worked for your co-worker may not work. There is no win or lose here. Keep going until something fits. Remove the lack. It is not our truth. It is not our voice.

New Voices

Once we decide what that is, it's time to let in some new voices. This comes with a heavy trial and error phase. It might be reading, journaling, yoga, meditating, podcasts, or fill in the blank. This is why we can no longer stay victims. The information is everywhere and comes in all shapes, sizes, voices, and stories.

Finding something to speak to areas I needed growth around was never an issue. Once I found it, I took in as much as I consistently could. It is hard to move the needle on the voice in our head if we aren't coming at it daily. The head moves everything so it is behind every vibe shift and belief.

I loved podcasts early on because it was a consistent voice that allowed me to process some things while working. Not everyone's job allows for that, but that was my jam early on. I had never thought of options outside of corporate. That was the best life promise I was given growing up. Go to college and find a steady corporate job. So that was a lack for me. I didn't know anything about other options. So I stumbled around and finally found the Don't Keep Your Day Job Podcast with Cathy Heller. She had a massive amount of episodes, so I loved being able to tune in once a day and get my mind wrapped around other options for making a life. She would show me things I couldn't unsee and became a voice to push me towards what I knew I wanted in life. Find what fits best, and just so you know, it is okay to outgrow it. Keep finding what you need to fill the lack gaps that exist. You will be amazed at what you find just stepping forward.

Trying to fix everything at once is a good way to burn out quickly. I like to see the cascading impact of fixing one thing at a time. But wherever can we find the time? Well this is where the importance of not being a victim takes over. If you wanted to, you would, so go find some space.

What needs to go that isn't helping you grow right now? What can take its place? How do we make it a habit to work on this part of our minds? What you will likely realize is that over time, your focus and commitment to the work frees up more time for more work. Start with as small of steps as possible.

Maybe it is just listening to good things on your commute. Maybe it is just reading something right before bed. So start with getting a consistent five minutes a day. Show up for that relentlessly and then see where else you can take it. Vary the intake. There are some things I can read and there are some things better spoken. You will know what hits you right.

However space is made, it's not what it is as much as it is that it's done.

THE
REALIZATION

CHAPTER SIX

Phase One

Realization

We've all heard of or even joked about these moments in life. Where, all of a sudden, we turn a certain age or have a minor meltdown about where we've found ourselves in life. This is the first phase I call realization. Sometimes it is a dramatic realization, sometimes it is a rather seemingly insignificant end to a chapter. The varying levels are really what is important. This phase either sent me out into the world crying "the sky is falling" or it came and went rather insignificantly.

No matter how it comes and goes, I was always finding myself at the realization again. The one that told me this is not right. This is NOT how it's meant to be. You deserve something better. Sometimes this just looks like searching for a different job and sometimes it looks like ending a lifetime career. I believe the bigness of it depended on my readiness for it. My acceptance of the judgment that was sure to come my way. My acceptance of the growth that would have to come along with it. Acceptance of the hard identity crisis that would follow. None of that really matters. What matters was that I found what didn't fit. I had come back to this realization in life. That meant it was time to turn the page in this book meant to be my story.

Most people refer to this lovingly as a midlife crisis. I had a midlife crisis-ish. I wasn't old enough to be in the "mid" zone of my life, but I was beside myself. I had made a comfortable plan and planned on that lasting most of my life. I was resenting this phase. I just wanted to be okay. I just wanted this job to fit. I didn't want to bounce around anymore. That didn't matter. The more I fought my realization, the more it fought back.

Eventually, it wouldn't give me a choice. I would cycle back to realization, trying to make this job or that fix fit, and nothing did it. I was always coming back knowing that this was not going to be enough. This was not where I was meant to be.

I would like to take a moment and point out that this is not some phase to laugh off with friends. That inkling in our gut that is telling us it's time...well, it's there for a reason. So, as much as society has made a joke of these moments, they are real. They are real and really meant to move us. Move us to do the work of our life. To remember what it was like to work in this world rhythmically, passionately. This is supposed to be the moment that shakes us awake. This is where people shake out of their daze and explore something new.

Maybe this book will prompt that shake. Even if it doesn't, I hope at the very least it builds a new awareness of the repeating phases of life. So people feel less concerned with cycling back to this moment of realization.

I want to normalize that. I have spoken many places, and most successful people will comment how what I was speaking about was so true and so normal. They go on to tell me stories about all the reinventions of the life they experienced.

It is quite lovely to have people find truth in what I talk about. It also pushes me to talk more about it. I was prepared in my middle-class upbringing to find one thing and stick to it. Anything outside of that known path would be unknown and I should certainly avoid it at all costs. So when life threw me a curveball and kept returning me to this realization, I was certain the sky was falling in and falling directly on me.

The sky is not falling. The sky is fading in and out for us, but it's unwavering. It is time that we look at the return to this moment. That we see it as what it is. It is not just a phase that will pass. It is a phase that is meant to last, meant to shake us out of sleepy patterns of existence. This life is meant for beauty, passion, and intelligence. Realizations are good for reminding us of that.

Investigate and remember what it was like to feel that way in your life. How you showed up for yourself and your passions. This phase wants us to wake up. So let's start to remember where we showed up as our best selves. What did we do? Who were we? How did we move through the world? Remember what that lightness felt like. Let yourself go back to that feeling. Close your eyes and feel yourself there. What kind of person were you before the world told you who you could be? How did you operate? It is good to remember those things here in the realization phrase because it is much lighter than what follows. Swim around in this dream-like state for a while.

Knowing what is not for us is vital. It is okay to realize that this job, career, company, or life choice is not for us anymore. From there, we can start to piece together what it is about, whatever it is that has gotten you to this realization. Take it out as granular as needed and get specific about what it is. What is missing from this part of life? What are the things you remember about your being and why doesn't this environment work? This starts to at least set a direction.

Even if we don't know where we want to end up yet, this is a great shift in frequencies. This is the start of something different. I know it seems counterintuitive to state the things we don't want to get, but trust me on this one. What isn't right is so many steps closer to establishing what is. Also, it helps later when we reach beyond phase two to remind us what all the fuss was about anyways.

I have always been grateful to have my podcast as the great reminder for me. When I was feeling lost, I always had it as a timestamp and reflection of the work I had already done.

I was lucky enough to voice what didn't fit on my show. It was a vital process of getting it down somewhere, this could have looked like journaling, which it inevitably was for me. That way when I needed a reminder, I had it and the physical exchange of words created action. But first, I had to take it out of my head and get it on paper, video, text, or my favorite podcast. I just had to let it all out.

Material Girl

I had exhausted my ability to let it fade into the material. One of the cruel human things we do is play to the material. It's that "grass is greener" type of philosophy. If I could just make more money, I would be happy at this job. If I could drive a nicer car, I would be fine with the commute.

You will never have enough of what you don't really need. - Matthew Kelly

The material was not what was lacking. And while all of these things would have been nice...I knew it wasn't going to do it. I knew if I took the easy way out I would be back here AGAIN. Looping and longing for more meaning. For a life as bright as I knew it was meant to be for me. I had to stop defaulting to the material. I struggled with this one a lot because I had reached those goals of mine. I thought this was just the next step. I thought people just upgraded until forever. I figured I would just keep getting raises and promotions and following those things. The goals that followed would be an upgraded car, house, clubs, and, well, everything until the money ran out...which would lead to the next call for ladder climbing and "necessary" pay increase.

If that's something you find very important, then by all means keep going, but it just didn't matter that much to me when I pushed back on it.

Most of the things I wanted were merely a societal expectation and projection of where I was "supposed" to be in life. So, if you are like me and it's not material then what? Well, that is what got hard about staying in corporate America. I lacked the want to hold onto the climb instinct that I should have gotten at business school. I liked money, but not for what it was costing, and it was costing me caring.

For a while, I threw all of that aside. I realized there wasn't room for softhearted weirdos in the world of business. Actually, in an interview for a healthcare system, I voiced that as a strength. I said, "My strength is being able to remove emotions from situations to just get the job done."

Now I suppose since I was on the business side of healthcare, it didn't matter so much that I basically just pointed out my ability to be heartless, but this was not a strength. It was something that actually took a lot of time to heal. I had to convince myself it was okay to feel again after I had spent my entire adulthood claiming it as my biggest asset.

The business world agreed. But truth be told, my feeling was what guided me, and while I had gotten good at turning it on and off easily in front of people behind the scenes, it took its toll on me. I couldn't understand why I just didn't fit right, but it was my sudden lack of need for the material. All of a sudden, the advancement didn't matter as much as the want to enjoy my job and make a difference. Once I saw how little of a difference I made and how much of my real self I had to hide, I didn't know how much longer I would have to convince myself this still fit.

The list of things there aren't have made their way somewhere at this point. So again we get to dream here. We get to feel what could be based on what isn't. One of my favorite parts of the book Untamed by Glennon Doyle is that she instructs readers to close their eyes and dream with no limits. Imagine unhindered. See what could be.

Now that we know what was holding us back, this gets easier. And now that we now know what it isn't, it gets easier still. I find uncovering those two pieces allows this to happen in a fearless state.

First, when I did this, those same voices that stopped all of my forward progress in the past perked right up again. Since my dream death had made a nice outline of the lies I had been telling myself I was already aware of their arrival. I had to have a conversation with those naysayers still stuck in my head. Mine sounded like, "I know that I have been told I am not smart and I may not have everything I need to make this dream happen, but I will find what I need along the way, don't worry."

I had those things pinpointed and mapped out before my fearless dream session. I wasn't expecting the need to be ready to release. The first time I did this, old versions of what had been wandered in. How I dressed, where I was currently in life and stature, and where I was working all found their way in. Those realities were attempting to point out how impossible this all was.

I politely dropped them at the door. We are talking about dreams that could fuel the rest of your life. I am guessing it looks quite a bit different from who we are right now and that is a beautiful thing. So prepare to let go of what has been and versions of our life we won't be able to take to this new one. I closed my eyes and opened them to a world of what could be. I got as specific as I could. When I closed my eyes, I could see my dressed-up tennis shoes resting atop a suitcase at an airport while I wrote and waited to board a plane. That brought up all of my limits, but I dismissed them and said this is just me and my dreams, not any of those limits and not likely any of the things I have been.

I now know that this is the top of the funnel. Throughout my life I had been in a constant cycle back to here. Each time a new phase, chapter, or season comes, I would find myself back here at realization. I like to think of it as a rebirth necessary for forward movement.

The cycle can take us as deep as we are willing to let it or it can stay superficial and keep repeating. This is our life choice. By the hundredth time cycling through I finally took time to slow down, make space, and start listening to it. I knew it was that or cramming my time full of what wasn't fulfilling. I wanted to show up caring for my life. I wanted to stand up for my needed presence and start living again. This wasn't just a phase or midlife crisis. This was sent here to shake me awake to bring me back to the mix of what life has come to be. I had to choose to go after what I could only see when I closed my eyes. I had to choose to be awake in life, versus silently suffering. I was not put here to slowly fade away. I was put here to shine in ways only I knew how. No one else will be prompted to take the exact same journey as me. No one has the skill set or background to tell the stories I can. I wanted to stop repeating phases, I was ready to stop pretending like a material possession or bonus was going to fix it all, so I closed my eyes and dreamt limitless. I wrote down all that I could see as far as it would take me. That day I couldn't unknow. Those dreams I could never unsee.

CHAPTER SEVEN

Wonderful & Terrible

Loop

Once I got started, it got worse. This part is a revolving loop.
Parts of the early realization phase feel like a million pounds
being freed. Other parts feel like walking in mud, with a
weighted vest and weights around your ankles. Most of it feels
wonderful and terrible all in the same breath.

Eventually when working on dreaming new dreams we make it
past the heavy doubt part, so we start to feel invincible. I was
so "high" on this I started telling people my dreams. I quickly
remembered that I wasn't past this part yet. While the high feels
awesome, I remembered the low quickly. I spent days in bliss
and weeks in exile. Every part of me wanted to retreat from my
current life, but it wasn't the right time yet.

I was grateful that I wasn't in a position to make any drastic
dream moves here. I had so much belief left to build before I
was vibrationally set to make that leap. A leap from here would
have left me desperate, vulnerable, and willing to do anything
to make any part of my dream happen. I knew it wouldn't last
like that. So even though it hurts, it was worth getting past. My
life up to this point looked like running at anything that felt like
freedom as fast as I could. Careless, consistent, focused, and
every time I got to running, I would be brought down by the
same old beliefs. If people's comments didn't stop me, my own
would before I could even get off the ground. I had started and
stopped about five different side jobs I wanted to try. Once the
motion would get rolling, I would freak out and stop every time.
This is why my realization at age thirty was so earth-shattering.

I refused to start and be stopped by these voices again. Outside and in.

It's a lot like raising kids. The most wonderful and terrible venture you will ever be on. Kids are amazing and terrifying. They are the ultimate test with no tangible result. The work is never done, the growing, loving, and nurturing never really ends. That's this work. While parts of it get easier and the voices grow softer, there is never a moment that passes where you graduate from self-discovery. The voices fade but never disappear. It is the best thing you ever decide to do, but it is the worst all in the same breath. I only point this out so you don't over romanticize either idea. Self-discovery or kids. Both worth every minute put in. Both equal parts terrifying and mystical.

It is this shift that hurts. It is this feeling of wonderful and terrible. Not as much as the fact that I was digging up painful parts of my past, even though I was. It was that my body wore out after a while. It wanted to be pain-free, and this process was forcing it. My mind was trying to heal while it opened closed wounds. This is complicated and messy and, quite frankly, downright terrifying. I think it's why we stay in the top two phases. The processing and movement forward are too dramatic of shifts. It takes so much mental and physical strength that most can't process by the time we are ready to do the work.

The ability to stay as shifted as possible for as long as possible is vital. Once I set out to figure this part out, I had decided at least one thing. That one thing was that I was going to figure out some dreams worth dreaming. I was not going to end up at the top in ten years listless again.

So I sat one morning listening to loons bring up the sun on the porch of a quant A-frame cabin on a small lakefront in Minnesota in front of my college laptop computer. I wanted so badly to get it right this time. I took my birthday off that year. One of the first birthdays I had spent outside of a gym since I was in 3rd grade. I decided I needed this time.

The whole four-day weekend I committed to this goal of figuring out my life. A couple books and a laptop were going to have to do the trick. I read enough to convince myself I had learned something applicable and started to write dreams down. Those dreams felt a lot like the old ones had. They seemed fine but it was nothing that reminded me of the passion I once felt on a court. They were fine. It would be fine. We would build a house. We would go on vacations. I would get a leadership role.

I looked at that list and fondly remembered the potential, guts, and lust for life I used to possess. What had done me in? Must have been the kids, responsibility, the need to provide food, shelter, heat, and water for someone outside of myself. So I wrote dreams down. Apple keys aflutter. I took a couple of photos to commemorate it. I laugh at it every time it comes up in memories on my birthday.

Two years after the photo was taken, I went back and actually read those books. The books on that trip were just a pawn so people would believe I was the kind of person who read and practiced self-development, but it was a mere facade. While I was writing dreams, they had no depth or breadth or any semblance of excitement to them for me. They would do what my dreams had done before...leave me bored and all the more anxious than I had been before.

That weekend I spent half pretending and half wholeheartedly wanting to come up with new dreams was not a waste. That was the vital vibration shift for me. It didn't matter whether I got it "right" or "wrong." The only thing that mattered was the shift I had created by openly stating that I wanted more. After that day, I incessantly moved toward this goal of creating/moving towards dreams. The dreams changed as I grew more curious about my life in this work, but the frequency of wanting something different never did, and that might have been enough to start and keep the shift headed in that direction.

Commandments

My upbringing was in a lower-middle-class home/town in the middle of the Midwest. This meant a couple of things. As discussed, dreams were usually just for a select few. Most of those few are not likely to be me. Money didn't grow on trees. As well as this overwhelming understanding of the importance of keeping the peace while face-to-face. No use ruffling any feathers. These were like an immovable set of truths. If there was a set of commandments for someone's life these were mine.

Commandment I: IF you make it out, you are free to run. If you don't, this will be your life sentence.

Commandment II: Money doesn't grow on trees, so there is no backup plan if you mess this up. Commandment III: Maybe it is just best if you toned it all down.

I had collected this list over the years. I can now thank it for guiding me perfectly to this place. For this portion of the work, I cursed it. Usually, my realization phase brought me back to my three commandments (I guess The Bible gets ten, I only needed three) and they always talked sense back into me. That sense led perfectly to the anger phase until I looped back again.

I would have never been aware of this mindset and how destructive (now known as divinely guided) it had been on my life path if I hadn't pushed myself to dig all the way in. If I hadn't gone ahead and surrendered to how I really felt. All of my past attempts at escaping were likely failing because of inconsistency.

Inconsistency caused by a foundation of beliefs that were untrue.

They were shaky at best. When I went to pick those ones apart, they crumbled in my hands. I think now about how many decisions I let those commandments own throughout the course of my life. All for them to crumble upon the first attempt to question their validity. That happened so often for me it was ridiculous. The moment I would track one truth back, I would stand sad but usually in the rubble of a useless belief.

Once I got past the darkness of reliving that moment, I could walk away unchained. Knowing the source let me release it. I could finally discover my truths. Truths worth walking towards. Truths worth living for. That mindset piece is easy to hand over to society, to geography, or to family/upbringing. This has to be where the phrase, "You are as strong as the five people you surround yourself with" (wouldn't be a self-discovery book if I didn't quote that) comes from. But I found there is life-changing work on the other side of examining what is yours and what isn't.

Commandment I: I believe in everyone's right and ability to dream.

Commandment II: Money may not grow on trees, but my abundance is overflowing looking no further than my breath.

Commandment III: I am best turned ALL the way up.

Silence

Surviving the silence of this work was the hardest for me. Words, beliefs, and goals are completely in my skill set, wheelhouse, everything. They are my jam. PERIOD. You would not have to ask me twice if invited to that party. But that isn't it. I wanted to believe, sitting on a quiet cabin porch, the serenity and goal planning would do it. Check the box, drop the mic, and walk on out of that peaceful escape.

That wasn't it. That wasn't it at all. I had to start making actual space for this work. A weekend mostly planning a post about "the work" I had done wasn't enough. For whatever reason, this felt so different than anything I had done before. I felt this overwhelming pull to drop stuff. To just stop with all the noise and let things settle down for the first time in my adult life.

As someone completely consumed with the belief that everyone cared that I was the busiest and most successful mom they had ever met, this voice was beyond annoying. I could not even consider that as a feasible, doable, or realistic plan whatsoever. So I held onto things too long, created pain I did not deserve, and eventually listened. After planning goals that were dumb and even less inspiring than the ones I had already achieved, I decided to listen to the voice and I started thinking about dropping volleyball. Altogether. This was a hard identity to give up. More than that, it was hard to think about opening that much time up. Time that I could commit to my family and myself. Both of these premises terrified me.

Volleyball court = definitive results. You perform or you don't. Done. Easy.

Corporate work world of marketing strategy = definitive, measurable results. Your analysis/recommendations perform or they don't. Done. Easy.

Family = never-ending, undefinable measure of whether you are doing it right = impossible, anxiety provoking, scary.

Quiet time = impossible, anxiety-provoking, not for me.

So that was what I committed to when I started taking time back that I wasn't even sure I wanted. I was committing to the unknown, the scary, the unapproachable. I was going to do this with my life after spending about ten years making fun of people who had this.

There I was, sitting with an unsettling, stripped athleteless identity for the first time in my life. There was no visible way of winning anymore. No one sitting and keeping score. I had to sit in the silence of my decision. I had to start fading from places I used to exist. I had to become invisible to the rest of the world to finally see myself. That was what it took. Me and my family known as the core four navigating this new and wobbly legged attempt to discover myself. What I would learn is that family doesn't keep score and there is no way to win. That initially scared me but I found it to be the only safe space for me to grow. Soft and scoreless.

While I thought the outward appearance of winning was what was important, I found the inward way of discovering what winning was to me. The silence. Well, silence and I still fight one another from time to time. There are days where Commandment III takes hold and throws silent practices out the window, but for the most part, I have learned this. Everything that needs the ground to grow is there. Silence gives me space to take my thoughts and delicately place them where they belong.

I would always rush in to say "who has time" or "must be nice to have time" (as passive aggressively as possible) or "yeah, meditating and silence...that's just not for me."

I would find it is for everyone who wants to take in life in the present moment as it is meant to be enjoyed. I can breathe with silence, and I make space to take silence in now. I realize the noise was just a distraction from the actual ability to position myself to win. If I was always busy, loud, and bustling, there was always a reason I couldn't get it all done. Business became the ultimate scapegoat and no one could or would ever question it. She is busy. She does do a lot. Off the hook. But silence put me in a position to keep and make more aligned agreements. I was no longer rushing to add another thing to keep up the facade of an identity I had created. This finally felt real. Meaning silence and family, the two things sure to push me overboard, saved me.

As quickly as I had arrived, I wanted to be freed. Right when I felt better, I was ready to run myself ragged all over again.

I remember coming back from my four-day trip refreshed and ready to ignore voices and run until I couldn't anymore. I had spent some time in silence. I had spent some time with my family. I had read five pages of each of the five books I brought with me on the trip. I wrote dreams. I played in the water. I did nothing. CHECK. Done with all the discovery. This was what I told myself because running just felt more natural and being brutally honest, running was the only thing that ever got me recognized.

So, I checked back in and went off to the races. Ignoring silence and family and doing what I do best, avoiding completely anything that might not have a trophy at the end. I was a real catch, let me tell you. This was all fine except I had already set the ball in motion. On my birthday, I had decided I didn't want these things anymore and the universe was already putting that into motion.

Deciding what you don't want is enough of a decision for the universe to make moves for you. So as badly as I wanted to outrun it and get a game plan together, I couldn't. The ball was rolling. Once the ball or goal or announcement is set in motion, there isn't a whole lot of taking it back. I always found more discomfort the more I tried to deny what I said I wanted. That is why this is not a start-and-stop endeavor. This is life. It is fluid and in motion. What you think about, you bring about, times infinity.

So once my ball was rolling, I found that I could roll with it or resist it, but the end result would be the same. Only the exits proved to be different. One was clean, concise, and abundantly aligned. The other was messy and painful. I still choose the messy and painful from time to time. I am still getting better at taking the first exit when prompted, but there are times where I still miss it.

The key is to just keep going and growing. I found that once I could quantify the phases, it made them easier for me to recognize the ending and new beginning that much sooner. This allowed me to move from trying one thing to the next a little quicker and less painfully. We are all a continued reinvention of ourselves. The seasons are meant to change. I only wish that I had forgiven myself sooner. I wish that I had not thought of my life as less than because of my one failure to become a division one athlete.

I realize I am an extremist and some might say to just get over it already. Pain is pain. Our stories, truths, and lies are ours and ours only. No one gets to come in and say what that is or can be for us. We decide now until forever. While I would never undo anything I have done because it is all amazing, I would have offered myself love instead of threats and acceptance instead of less. One slip up doesn't end the whole story. Neither does one redirect or seven. It is an ever-evolving part of your story. One more step to take us where we were meant to be all along. This is unwavering.

Dots

I want this part to be known as hard and frustrating upon each passing revolution, but also know it is a part of the evolution story to look back on and draw lines to. It isn't meant to make sense in the messy middle part of it all. It will only make sense when we look back and connect all the dots of our life back up. So I just started living. Saying what I wanted and accepting nothing less.

That doesn't happen without pulling out the messy past and making sense of some of those dots. The dots weren't meant to stop me as much as they were meant to guide me to exactly where I was. I thought the death of my dream was the death and end of me, but that dot point is one of the most important points there will ever be.

Upon close, both wonderful and terrible, examination, it seemed like a sticking point that left scars. That dot was the single dot that allowed all of these dots, and while it was painful, it also became purposeful, and that is what connecting the dots can tell us. Make us aware of that which we would have never known. Make us do things that don't line up at the present moment but will make sense later. That is all this is. Finding what fits in each present moment, knowing that one day all the dots will come into play.

I believe we are all here for a reason and we all have the same opportunity to figure out what that reason is. Some choose to find it and connect all the dots while others are buried with it. I just wanted to find my say in it all. Even if it was a terrible experience to explore, wouldn't just the chance be wonderful? It can all be weighted and balanced or we can just start living it. Choosing our life and making it all happen. Life is wonderful and terrible all in the same breath. I chose to default to wonderful. Both existing but choosing one as the higher percentage to the other. How can we get more curious about what would make our life even more wonderful? I don't think we need to entertain the other.

THE RAGE

CHAPTER EIGHT

Phase Two

Spin

I had spun myself too far this time. I hated myself and my life even more than before. In my mind that meant this self-work stuff wasn't working. My disinterest in life worried me the most. I had given up everything I thought I ever wanted and I was left wandering and lost.

I had attempted to start writing and doing the things I half assedly acknowledged. I had spun around and stopped all forward motion for the fourth time. I was beat down. I had nothing. I was nothing in my eyes. Nothing stuck.

One day I was listening to a podcast by Cathy Heller, Don't Keep Your Day Job is the name of it, and they kept asking: Where do you light up? What would you do for no money at all? Which, at the time, I most certainly scoffed at that suggestion. But I did it anyway, and it prompted me to start paying attention to that for the first time ever.

What did I enjoy? What did people come to me for? It was at least a scent to start sniffing for because all of my attempts to hate myself into action just hadn't worked. I can't imagine why. So I started to pay attention to the highs and lows. What made some days light up like fireworks and others dark as night? It took a while to track, but I wrote down variances and started to see the trend. Mornings that I spent on the phone helping a family member talk something out always sparked my entire day full of energy. So, for a while, I was dependent on family members to bring me back to enjoying my life.

Eventually they ran out of problems and stopped answering the phone. So I was back to the low days. But I had found something consistently light for the first time. When the phone calls stopped, I just started having these conversations with myself and I recorded them. I wanted to see if the light followed even when it was just me. It did. The energy repeated over the phone or a recording. I figured someday it could be a podcast, but I didn't have any clue how to do that, so I just kept recording. Not because I thought I was going to eventually make a podcast, because it just felt better. It was like a release for me that I had not felt in a very long time.

I made the conscious decision to just make it how I knew how. So it was three months of audio files that were sent to a select group of friends who never responded. The crickets worried me but it didn't matter. Again, this just felt better. I wasn't going back to doing nothing. Whether or not anyone would listen wasn't the point.

I learned how to publish a podcast and leaned on a girl group that formed from my conference to force my first published podcast in July 2019. They were actually excited for me. It was terrible. I didn't know how to edit, I had basic/free equipment, and I couldn't piece audio together or add music. I am sure people had higher expectations, but it was all that it could be. I knew nothing, but I was trying.

In the beginning, I just set out to be as real as what was happening. My life was a mess. I was questioning every single thing I had built my life and beliefs around. I had a whole plan for my life that I was actively ripping apart and dissecting in real time on my podcast. It was a rather insane way to experience it all, but it was the only thing that kept me going and the only thing that made me feel better. There are so many pieces I wish I didn't live out loud. So many things that I might consider doing over or saying differently. It was a mess. It was real. It was me in all my dream rebuilding glory. Real, raw, and raging.

My sister-in-law Jasmine and I were shopping one weekend and we were rolling some jokes around. She said she had met a guy and he could really use my podcast. I laughed. Then she said, "I think I would just warn him about the first season."

She would be right to do that. It was a wild, real-time experiment. It was like Truman Show stuff except I knew I was doing it. I smiled and said, "Yeah, season one needs an asterisk, but at the same time it was my truth and if someone is experiencing what I did, it will probably be theirs as well in a sense."

It's just messy. There is no way around it. The reconstruction of a life...is season one messy. So messy that I was listening to a lot of southern authors' audio books at the time and started implementing a terrible southern drawl. I have no idea why.

I don't know how long I did it, but I thought for a little while my southern accent would be like my pen name. IT would be my pen voice. I don't know why it happened, but it is included in all the messiness. I had been without identity for so long I guess I held onto whatever I tried on in that season.

I once thought about going back to edit season one, clean it all up, and put some intros on, but I never have. I wanted the show to evolve with me. To see the show grow with me. I wasn't all that sure I would ever heal myself. Midway through season two, I was certain I just created an entire podcast that was a lie because I was ready to throw it all down the drain. Dreams and all. But I found my way when I was growing weary.

Rage

The show started out mostly in the rage portion of my phases. I had weighed out what I wanted to do, tried on a few, and the podcast stuck, so it became the thing. Not because I had any sort of support, and rightfully so.

I call the audio files recorded from April-July the dark files. They contain a lot of expletives and more anger than I even had in the first season. I had toned it down for the podcast, I will say that. So the people who reviewed them and didn't respond likely put in a call to my friends and family to make sure they were checking in on me. Also rightfully so.

A good portion of the blame I had for my life at this point was related to my sex. I was a female. That was a topic that was covered angrily and in length on the show. All of the reasons I hadn't gotten things because of my sex. To say the very least, I seemed feminist AF. In the heat of my show, I would cuss a lot. This felt better than the movement that needed to happen next. This was the blame and anger portion where everyone but me was responsible for what happened, and it felt good being able to point the finger and run. Or yell at a microphone and drop it. I am sure this could not have been left unexpressed. There is something therapeutic about getting it all out on paper, or venting, or however, but the conversion of the toxic energy is important. Venting has its proper places and I can almost promise everyone that its proper place is not in a daily podcast. But it was needed. I needed to be able to point every single finger I had to show myself even when the dirty laundry was aired, the only thing left was me.

I sort of became even more toxic than I was before. Now I had an outlet where I could exist, and it boosted me and my ego up for the first time in a while. It felt good to just say F all the way off, haters don't get it and they never will. That was my approach. If someone couldn't see what it could be, they were labeled as jealous or not smart enough to understand the art of podcasting. This made me a bit of an outspoken Iowa outlaw. An open and angry mouth from a woman broadcasted places...this is not what good Iowans do. The version of Iowans I knew best were work hard, head down, and collect a paycheck, so this was a blatant disregard of that and made me stick out everywhere. I was proud, but also aware that I might also just be insane, and walking that line made it easy to keep it tight to my chest.

I was at a book reading by an Iowan author who writes on the interesting and mostly unknown history of Iowa. She said in her talk that Iowan's have the same interesting history as most everywhere else, but Iowan's just don't write books or produce movies about it. That's just not what Iowan's do. I agree. We keep things pretty close to our chests. It might be the tiny towns where people know more about you than you know at times. Who knows. But I felt like that was even more of a reason to keep going. Tell a story from a perspective not often heard from. Never mind the fact that I was a jerk about it but whatever. We now understand this to be a part of the process so...forgive me, I knew not what I was capturing.

In true Iowa tradition, I did what was asked of me. I kept my head down and my mouth only heard on a podcast I did not promote unless asked about. I still don't know how the show spread as quickly as it did. Other than probably most people shared it to make fun of it or just listen to the dumpster fire of a show it was. People couldn't look away, I guess. I am so thankful for my ego at this time. It came in and protected me from stopping. It propped me up just high enough to know to keep going anyways.

Iowan at heart, I just let it play out, half expecting to never have an interesting story to tell and half expecting to stop after I got tired of it three months in. But the energy kept repeating. At some point, I had to change my morning routine to fit the podcast in before work. So my wake-up time became 3:30 am to get the show done, myself ready for work, kids off to school, and myself to work on time. Still the energy repeated. I never felt tired a single day that I showed up on the microphone. I was still angry at the world, openly taking shots, and exploring all the ways the world had done me wrong for most of the first year. The rage/ego fueled me through what happened next.

Rage Against All the Machines

The awareness of my show had started to spread. Slowly like in any good small town. Rumors spread. People would come up and say the craziest things. Most conversations started like, "Ya, I listened to your podcast..." awkward silence always followed. They just wouldn't say anything at all. This happened a lot. I mean, I understand now it was just terrible and there likely wasn't a set of words to lean on to describe it to someone's face no less the creator.

People would also come up and say things like, "I have ideas... can I just start a podcast." Or one of my personal favorites, "Ya, it seems like everyone has a podcast now."

This helped to fuel even more rage than before. People were adding to the fire and it was already burning. I am sure this is where a lot of blood was shed. If I didn't burn bridges before the show, I definitely did in the first season. Listen, I was mad and then I felt attacked. That does not make up for anything I did or said, but it was just a part of things I had to work through. For the most part, people became an easy way to avoid taking the next step in this work. The more people made comments, the more I had to attack and highlight my anger, leaving me hanging in the balance lacking forward motion. Which is what I preferred.

So I was searching for machines to rage against. If you had any fraction of a doubt or misstep in comments about my work...you were exiled. I had no use for people adding to my already overflowing list of self-doubt. So, goodbye. It was quite easy to dismiss people. Left more room for my thinking and processing. I pointed out and spoke to everything I believed in. I raged against corporate structures, leaders, status, feminism, algorithms, race, my upbringing, and the tininess of the place I found myself sitting in. If there were ways to do this, I assure you I was not doing it the preferred way.

It was insanely hateful. It left many wounded in my wake. In my mind, I was providing the best service possible. I was saving people from these unknown evils, but I wasn't. I was obsessing about concepts and letting myself off the hook. So long as we discussed it, we are doing a good type of work.

May I never find myself in those meeting rooms again. Where truths are swept under the rug to keep the people in power happy and still in power. I could rage on anything. People at my corporate job found it quite entertaining. I would sometimes be invited on projects just for my voice. Just for my unknown. If something needed stirred up, I was the best woman for the job. I was disruptive and found a new level after the podcast because I now had the ability to move words in a more succinct way.

There was never a shortage of reasons to rage in my line of work. Healthcare. If there was a cause to fight for or against, I was in it. If there were opportunities to lead as a change agent, I rushed at the chance. There was a way to make it better and I knew how, or I at least wanted the chance to.

When I wasn't given a chance, I began to rage even more. The gloves were off at this point. I was working through everything I had ever known and trying to figure out where I wanted to fit in this world. Was this my dream? Healthcare had been, but was it still? I didn't know the answer, but my only option was to spin and fight and rage in any room I was welcomed in.

Healthcare seemed slow moving and untouched to me. Like the perfect storm of an industry to be disrupted. That charge I wanted to lead. The needed change I desperately wanted to be a part of.

Since healthcare just was what it was and Iowa just was what it was, the doors I was so hellbent to knock down pushed back. I am certain I cried on the podcast at one point because I just wanted a chance. I was frustrated and bewildered. Nothing had ever taken me this long to master and move up, and if I was being honest, I didn't even know what I wanted. Since I was just in a blind rage for what seemed like an eternity, I couldn't function well anywhere. At home, I was exhausted from bright, aligned mornings and dark, angry days. The highs and lows took a toll. How could the two worlds both exist in the same one?

On the microphone, I felt angry but in flow and alignment. In my day job, I felt angry but in spite and disruption. There were parts of me that felt that healthcare was my only option and my calling. Maybe I was sent here a disrupter and the only way for me to find my path was to jump in it and stir it up. Either way, that way of work was exhausting and not true to my natural being. This was me working in my darkness. It was drama. It was spite. It was blame. While this all felt like a normal day, at this point there was something I could tell that wasn't right with it. I was forcing the fit.

Most days I spent in rage felt wild and unnerving. Nerves would always send me to places where I felt in control. That usually involved a splurge shopping spree or a binge eating daze. I had no control over my emotions. They were running my mouth and the show. I was a big dose of extra, which was what I wanted, but I also wanted to be able to scale it back when needed. At that point, emotions were running every show and the commercials.

There was no escaping the extreme bigness and smallness I was operating in minute to minute. The only escape seemed to be excessive amounts of shopping. I was an active and good consumer who was also an early adopter, so I had all the new things months before people even knew they existed. It was fun to be so well informed on all things material. There was a level of cool that I couldn't even begin to explain. So that was my fix. I would rage, throw fire unaware of the damage or consequences, and then tap out to take blissful control again. Wandering and establishing dominance wherever I could. It was very much a rage, buy, repeat model for longer than we could honestly afford. So long as I always had something to take my mind off whatever hell I had drummed up for myself on Monday, it was fine.

Weekends were filled with unpleasant activities and shopping. Weekdays were filled with overwhelming roller coasters of emotions. Weeknights spent overthinking every word said over the course of that day.

I was never fully there. I was always thinking about the wreckage left by my fits of passion and anger. Always watching my back with every word. To the world, seeming egotistically bold, but to me, knowing I was anxiously out of control. Nothing a weekend of consumption couldn't fix.

Luckily for everyone, my addictions were kept that simple. Not everyone is so lucky. No one seemed concerned, so neither was I.

Even with this deep knowing that something was wrong, I kept pressing on because questioning life at this point seemed rather out of my league. I felt I was too young to question where I was "supposed" to be or if this passed down "normal" way of living was for me or not. So I just kept spinning back and forth between realization and anger every day for about eight months. Each day leading me to the realization this isn't fitting or is spinning me into fits of anger, always pointing out my lack of control over my life and inability to change it.

The comfort I felt there was enough to keep me in it. The next step of figuring out how to move past the anger seemed too daunting. Even if I was forever spinning, at least I know what I am doing here. At least people find me funny here. This groove would be hard to leave because even if I resented it, it fit.

I knew I wanted something else but feared what I would have to leave if I went looking. But the shopping wasn't curing the pain anymore. I was just in self-induced pain. There was no relief that worked. The podcast was the only thing that pushed me to step past this moment and start looking beyond the horizon of what

I could make happen. Even if no one was listening, I knew I had to do something about this for myself. I knew I couldn't stay here forever. I knew I needed to transition. I knew I needed to take back control on more than just shopping trips and eating binges. I knew I needed to start leading my life and determine the destination.

THE EGOLESS
SELF DISCOVERY

CHAPTER NINE

Ego

Leaving the Loop

The biggest hurdle to overcome was getting out of the rage/
anger mode. Actually, bailing myself from that loop was the
issue. The loop was comfortable. It was easier. Everything in that
loop fit me. Until one day it didn't.

All of a sudden, I had this epiphany that was like a lightbulb
went on and never turned off again. I could no longer look at
the world the same way ever again. I heard whatever I heard
one million times in a million different ways (that is why I like
podcasting so much because lightbulb moments take time,
repetition, and luck in the landing) and that day, for whatever
reason, this hit me like a bag of bricks.

There I was sitting at a company culture meeting that I was
helping to facilitate and these words were etched into my soul
that day. Experiences build beliefs, beliefs influence action,
action determines results. (Partners in Leadership). I was stuck
in the action-taking portion of life. Action was my comfort zone,
but I had been acting from old beliefs that I was working to
restructure.

So that day, I realized I would have to create some new
experiences around the new beliefs I wanted to hold. This
shouldn't have taken this epiphany. This was inevitably what
I did with greatness grounding with my State Championship
volleyball team three years before this moment. But the dots
aren't usually connected like that. I would realize that day the
life I was leading was operating two layers deep. Luckily, I was

raised in environments where working hard was the expectation, so I took a whole lot of action, but the reason it did and didn't stick was the old beliefs. My old beliefs were rooted in my ego. If my identity was dependent on who I was and how I was performing, then one could imagine how important it would be to constantly perform, raise a hand, solve the problem, be a part of the solution.

Ego is a person's self-esteem or sense of importance. So it is rather important. I had spent most of my life after the initial dream death at seven allowing other people to determine my sense of importance. This was my first test drive steering that ship on my own. So the jump took time, but finally quantitatively understanding where I was operating was a game-changer. My time was spent building a house with no known foundation. Each board shifting, bending, and breaking with each new job or person's determination of my worth. The new focus would become restructuring the foundation. Taking my time to intentionally place each board. Placing boards built to someday hold the house of my dreams.

Ego is this amazing thing. While it usually has a negative connotation, it actually is a protector. My ego shielded me from actual pain for years. It saved me from dealing with things I was not mentally ready to tackle. It would boost me up to take action and protect me when I fell back down again. But ego is also a great way to stay in the anger.

Ego was always telling me I was right. ALWAYS. That kept me safe in my own knowledge and made me feel confident in waging wars on people who came to question me. But my ego misled me, for I was not always right and I had no need to wage wars.

My ego told me the world was against me and I must rise up against anyone who looked like a threat. Tear them down. Break them down. Win the day. Which was fine as a competitor, but I began to see the world differently. I realized that nothing I did, said, or prepared for in competition mattered. It still always came back to me. My performance. I spent a lifetime propping my shattered self up on my ego avoiding any fault. It was always someone or something else. My ego had done a great job shielding me, but it was time for it to take a break. I needed to learn more than I knew. Let others speak and sit back for a bit to observe. My ego hated that right away. She reminded me of the scarcity and vulnerability that would lie on the other side. Ego wanted me to stay where I was out of fear of where I was going. Ego didn't know what would come next for that part of myself that meant we might lose it. It was a test in letting down my guard and letting people see a side of me that wasn't cutthroat and emotionless. This side had never really had a chance in this world.

At seven, my ego came in to save the day and I built a safe and scarce life around it. So I sat on my hands. I removed my voice. I was present and unwavering in my pursuit of removing my desperate need to shine. I dulled it up a bit. I stopped raising my hand. I let others lead. I let go of the strongest piece of me I had ever known.

This new view allowed me to look at everything from an accountable manner. The culture coach training I received was life-changing because this was the focus. The training walked us through how we transition our peers. Our job was to create a culture of accountability. I don't know about anybody else, but it clicked all the way for me. All of a sudden, I found myself raising my hand to be accountable for things I didn't even have any reason to be. Someone messed up the payroll, and even though I was in public relations, I probably had something to do with it.

It was funny because it opened my eyes to how often I glanced over my accountability for most things. I always had my guard (ego) up, so I was usually quickest to point the finger. It was never me. It was never my fault. That was how I handled the sports conversation as well. It was always easier to comment on a game ending injury than own what really happened. I was not good enough.

When I realized that I gave up, owning an injury for the rest of my life seemed a lot easier than owning a failure. So I pushed that off on knowing that I overdramatized and overextended an injury for an embarrassing amount of years. I suppose I wanted to make good on the story. More scars = more believable.

Ego instructed this constant need to keep myself safe, as if this world was always going to be against me. Which, most of my life growing up, it was, or so I was told. The world was scarce, there was never enough to go around. So I should make sure to take as much as I could get when I got the chance. I also knew there wasn't a possibility that I would get a second chance. So every time was probably the last time. I wasn't raised to believe in second shots. It was rather black and white. I was taught you win, you succeed. You fail, you lose. So my ego played overtime.

As a young athlete, my scarce mindset was always playing some story in the background. It was constantly telling me I was not enough and anyone who was had some unfair advantage or the referees on their side. This made me a real treat to play against and, I'm sure, coach. I didn't have anyone I would listen to even if they had tried to guide me. I had a whole lot of ego protecting me from the truth of my own insecurities. All guard, no gut.

This was okay. In the world of competition, it actually made me a "fierce" competitor. Likely the one that hyper masculine coaches dream about when coaching female athletes. But once I got to the real world, the skill set stunted my growth, and now looking back, it hurt my athletic growth as well. Ego told me I was the best, so there was no reason to let anyone else in. So I didn't. No one else ever knew better than me, and just like when I was a young athlete, anyone ahead of me cheated, slept, or privileged their way to the top.

I had convinced myself of my underdog status so much I'm not even sure looking back now if that was ever true. I wrote that story into my narrative so deep I think I actually created my own fall. Ego, guard, and this narrative of underdog was like a box I built myself into. While it felt safe to stay in, it was holding me back from greatness I deserved to experience. Ego told me to trust no one, to question everything, and at the end of the day, to only count on myself, but it lied. It misled me and it made me miss out on everything the world had to offer.

Scarcity

Ego is a scarce way to operate in this world. While it is needed at times to bolster up and move in boldness we may not be ready for, it is also misleading long term. It is a mixed-up mindset that caused me to move in ways I could never benefit from.

In the workplace, I attracted a whole lot of ego. People who hired me were likely in a similar mindset, so they liked my fire and fierceness. Ego made me remove my feelings because those were always distracting me from doing what I needed to do for me. Always about me and my needs over anyone else's.

At times, it left me teetering on the edge of narcissism. But I was doing what I needed to do to be successful in my mind, so nothing mattered but that, for my company and for myself. Ego constantly guided me to the one truth I held onto my whole life. This is it. This could be the ONE chance, don't let feelings get in the way. Don't let anything get in the way. Climb the ladder. Don't suffer forever. There may only be one shot. DON'T MISS. So I shut down everything and everyone.

My way was the only way. The only truth. The only thing I could ever trust. Ego also told me to only rely on me. No one else had my drive. No one else had my passion, insight, or understanding. I was a one-woman wrecking ball. Coming in with no feeling and leaving without it as well. Except I did feel.

What I hid in the workplace and on the court coaching were all of my truths nicely packaged and calmly not caring. When I got home, it was a different story. I would obsess and call and have to get all of the pent-up caring out. Nightly vent sessions with anyone who would listen. Anxiously spinning and overthinking until I could come up with a plan that placed me calmly back in control.

Guard always up, I couldn't let anyone see me slip. If I slipped, I might lose my chance. If I lost my chance, I would be back at square one. I would be a failure and people would see my weaknesses. Just keep going. Keep running. Keep smiling. No one will notice. You don't know if you never let any feelings show, I would convince myself.

So each night at home became a place to obsess over every detail anxiously. Not present, I would stew through the house, always too mentally exhausted to actually enjoy time with my family.

When I did spend time with them, conversations always revolved around maintaining my victim/underdog status. I created drama even when it didn't exist. Victimhood was a guard. It allowed me to operate safely under the umbrella of out of my control. Never was anything my fault. How could it be when I had all the right answers? I was a genius who was always misunderstood or didn't have the right degree or the right background or last name. This was the ultimate protection. I felt all of it. Every single emotion. Every high and low. Every time I painfully communicated in my rage that I would rather just end it all. Ego masquerading as my protector while it shuttered all of my opportunities.

I convinced myself I was fine and that this was the only way to operate in this world. The world was hard, cold, and careless. There was no room for emotion. The entire experience was supposed to feel this way. Mostly miserable, and once in a while something cool happens, but don't count on it. Pay taxes. Work. Die. That was the promise and so I didn't think that much of it when that was my experience.

It was as if the whole world was in on it. The turn of phrase "just living the dream" filled most pass by conversations where we all waited for the weekend to at least enjoy 20% of our week. I don't know why that one phrase always made my skin crawl. I am sure I vented on it to extreme extents on my podcast. I wanted to live the dream. I never really understood why we couldn't. Why our hallways were filled with people accepting this dreamless state as reality and why others weren't.

I chalked it up to again some victim mindset. I got stuck in Iowa (not actually, I could have left). Iowa is too small to do anything cool (we can all do anything from anywhere now...internet). We must all just have settled for less because only fancy people can make their dreams happen (they may have more training readily available or have started out ahead, but anyone can).

"Just living the dream" haunted me. Maybe it was my optimism or slight ADD or OCD tendencies, but I obsessed about this a lot. At that point, I was "living the dream." I was working, had everything I needed/wanted, and I spent most of my free time openly hating my life and most of the people in it.

This is what dreams are made of, I would convince myself. It had to be. This was all I had experienced. Raised in victimhood, protected and surrounded by scarce mindsets. This was all I had ever known and my ego wanted to make sure it was all I ever knew.

Presence

It always happens in December. I had been podcasting for a little under six months at that point and I was starting to realize how much of a difference this "work" was making. In me, not the world.

I was sitting in a meeting. I had just gone through training on accountability and was also doing some deep dives into ego. That day, I decided to go to a meeting to listen for the first time in my entire career. I was going to surrender to the present moment and force myself to actually listen. This may not seem earth-shattering to some people, but for me it was. It was the first time I was going to show up to a meeting, ego aside, and look to learn.

In most meetings, even if I didn't have the opportunity to speak, I wasn't listening. I was all up in my head. Most of the people who worked with me would comment or call it out knowing I was somewhere else cooking up a response or solution somewhere outside of where we were. So this showing up was drastically different. It was scary and everything I had ever known told me this was a sure-fire way to get looked over.

My ego would whisper in my ear that listening wasn't a good way to lead, it was just a good way to get lost. As scary as it was, I put ego aside for that meeting. I didn't plot, plan, or move out of the present. It raised more than a few eyebrows. I said nothing.

After the meeting, I got a call from a couple of bosses wondering if I was okay. I simply responded that I felt like everyone had taken the conversation where it needed to go and so there was nothing for me to add. It was my first time presently experiencing other people's opinions, not so scared that my intelligence would be questioned if I didn't interject, thus stealing me from the present moment.

This may have been the first time I ever valued anyone else's voice over my own. I think people started to worry. I know people started to worry. Their concern was that I was tapping out, but for the first time ever I was actually tapping all the way in. It changed the way I moved. I stopped polarizing and analyzing and just listened. This opened up all the learning. My ego had told me being the expert would protect me, so I had to market and protect that image at all costs.

Once it sat on the sideline for long enough, I saw that clinging to this identity robbed me from all that I could have been lucky enough to know. I wasn't going to let that happen anymore.

Whatever December does to me, it caused me to transition to a place of no return with this work. I couldn't go back to ego operation even if I tried. It felt as if I had graduated to a new level of operation.

Finding myself more in the present moment allowed me to stop worrying about the next steps, ladders, promotions, or demand that there was anywhere to go. I wasn't working to protect an identity. I was working for the pure sake of work and bringing and doing something beautiful in this world.

My focus and love for my work shifted a bit and it felt better. I felt like I was finally channeling energy appropriately and was feeling frustrated with my situation much less than before. There was a lot more stability in the present moment. I was home when I was home, listening and engaging in life there. It didn't feel as confusing because with ego removed there was nothing to win with family. Winning was my presence.

From that point, focus started to shift. I no longer set out to prove anything. That left me open to a whole new set of experiences. Things I never would have found worthy operating out of my ego. I found myself in and experimenting with more and more. While I was not perfect and still operating in and out of an ego place, overall it felt more stable. I could see myself showing up better in the places I cared about. I also felt myself showing up better for the people I worked and lived with on a day-to-day basis.

It was here that I had my first experience floating. I hadn't felt this light since I was a kid. Lightness that came from releasing this mindset that was holding me down my whole life. I was no longer living to escape. I was no longer presently un-present. I started to see myself in my life, and most importantly, I could finally see everyone else.

While it felt weird, it always felt better. I was finally able to see and own it all. I found a focal point that started the work of accountability. The surrender to my story led to the surrender of my ego, which was hellbent on saving me from the unknown.

Creating a life forced to operate anywhere but where I was. As much as I wished this was not my story, it was, and it became one I had to talk about to own the transition to something more fitting for me.

In order to dream, I had to believe I was deserving, which took disarming the alarm set to send me back into my scarce way of thinking. I found myself operating in a much more level state without my ego steering the ship. Far less calls to jump overboard and stay in my story even when storms started to brew. This was unlike any way I had ever experienced my own operation.

CHAPTER TEN

Self-Discovery

Self - Help

I used to be and still am obsessed with the "self-help" section of the bookstore. I suppose I could have gravitated to any section, but that was and has always been "it" for me. I would listen to my mom's Joyce Meyer cassette tapes with her in awe and read John Maxwell books through college like a philosophy scholar.

This was my section from a very young age. Most of the characters and books I read were more aspirational dreamer type works than anything. Beauty and the Beast was my favorite Disney movie, Molly was my chosen American Girl doll. Stories that revolved around someone who found themselves a little different from the rest of the world, but always had a dream and found a way.

My love for this genre was etched everywhere I looked when I started making my way back. It was nearly undeniable that there was something here, but in my work, I would also find another truth here. I would find that there was a wonderful and terrible piece to this. It was the name for me. Self-help.

After two years in that space, in some fashion I realized I didn't like the way this was named. The book companies must have agreed because around the time I was throwing it out they started to as well. Self-help became self-discovery and we all grew a bit together. Self-help stood for crisis and it always made me feel weird shopping in this section so often. It was as if something was wrong with me that I needed help with. Which, admittedly, something was, but committing the fact that I needed "help" increased the level of shame spiral I was already on when standing out in public shopping for books in this section.

I should have done what normal people do and comfortably shop for self-help from home, but I didn't, and the shame of this section burned a deep red on my cheeks. But I just liked it for the pure sake of liking it. I found these authors and thought leader from even my younger years to be quite amazing. It wasn't about the help to me. It was about the love and constant work we all have in this life to discover. So I changed the term and so did others. None of us should feel guilty or weird about the help, but help just isn't the right word for me. Should we go looking for teachers in this life who can help us prompt discovery, we should know they may have helped but we discovered. We choose to discover and apply. We chose to change.

This is the next essential phase. I lump everything in phase three all together even though we will take time to lay them out separately. The only reason is this phase didn't stand as distinctly alone as the others. It weaved too closely together for me to box it up separately. Self-discovery phase is a fun one because once we have broken down our old beliefs and laid our ego to rest for a little while, we can start learning for what may seem like the first time ever.

This is the part where you lay bricks side by side with your new beliefs that have taken hold. I had thrown a lot away and this is the first phase where I started adding some stuff back in. It felt good to be in a place of addition after so many seasons of subtraction. This part is where I learned all about me. Where I began remembering the love of inspirational words, creativity, and dreams. This is where I learned more about how my brain worked in mysterious ways. Phase three is more addition than subtraction. On the other side of ego, it is in a sense the first fun phase.

Restructuring beliefs is a vital piece of all of this. I had beliefs that held up parts of my full expression. So a lot of work teaches you to find yourself first. My experience with discovery taught me before the breaking down of beliefs movement and discovery weren't worth the work. That was my truth. I had waved in and out of believing in there being worth in the human I was constantly showing up as. I had learned to hate her and the rhythmic and inconsistent spurts she was commonly working in. I dreamt daily about how wonderful it would be to just sit down and unexcitedly get to work. Work. Work. Work. Force the fitting of something that was not true to how my brain worked.

In my beliefs, I found this to be an important/vital way of living. I was forcing the fit. There was a way that I wanted the world to see me and I had told myself it had to look this way or it would never be good enough. I believed there couldn't be worth in who I was, so I forced myself to become something completely different and it was draining. It was a shaky and untrue existence. It created darkness that eventually swallowed me whole.

Enneagram Seven

I am an enneagram seven. I used enneagram teachings most in this phase. There may likely be a more fad worthy self-discovery tool by the time you read this, so just know that was just "the tool" that was trending at that time. I believe in all the tools. I also believe in looking back at tools and tests you have used in the past if available.

I remember the day I took the free enneagram test. I got enneagram seven. I was sorta banking on getting an enneagram three. I got seven. There was disgust with that number at this stage in my life and also relief. It created this interesting juxtaposition that I would have never stumbled onto and yet I kind of had. I took more tests and read more books. I tried to convince myself I was something else and it ALL came back seven.

Since I had done work to discover some new beliefs, I had at least not thrown this discovery completely away like I would have in the past, at this point fighting it but openly aware of its importance. Being an enneagram seven meant I was joyful, adventurous, an enthusiast, and free. I could see sparks where that person existed. Mostly on vacation and burning bright and out quickly. Every piece of me was angry about this test result. If that was me, I had done this all wrong. I went looking for proof. I went looking for answers.

Ferociously, I ripped through boxes of things I collected from my youth. There was a big black binder that was going to show me the tests were wrong. I was counting on it. I didn't exactly remember what this binder had for content but I knew in middle school it was "the project." It was a career binder. It was filled with personality tests and career assignments based on that test. It also contained the reflection/interviews of people in those professions.

Before I opened it, I was certain this was going to tell me that enneagram seven was not right. I had even done a mild but effective study and collection of materials that told me how often enneagram tests were wrong. Either way, this binder was it. I opened the first page of perfectly preserved page protected information and found the exact opposite of what I was looking for. Based on all of my tests, I had settled on a career in photography. As I flipped through pages, I could see my carefully considered choice. While this was not my first, second, or third assigned career, I marketed to myself to make it make sense. This is what I wrote:

I choose photography as the best career choice for me based on my personality test because radio DJ, writer, and speaker are all too big of things that would be hard to make a living off. Photography is a career choice I could make happen.

At thirteen, the assignment was to find a career path based on personality testing and create a path for how you could aspire to that career. I couldn't see anyone who made a living off that (although I certainly could, I just had to consume content), but it was too far from reach to use as an actual example of possible for me. So I chose the only one I could actually see. This is why creatives must go out and stand proud in their art and possibility for kids who may never nurture a gift because no one is standing around them. We can be that one voice that says it's possible. Pursue. We never know who needs us.

Either way, I sat there stunned. At this point, I knew that my dream died at seven. I wasn't aware there was actual documented proof that I didn't believe what I wanted or even what tests would tell me I wanted. There it was in black and white, everything before this moment standing, memories foggy but becoming clearer. This was tangible. This was true. This binder confirmed it all. I was always an enneagram seven, but I spent most of my life lost or guided towards what was normal. What was easily accepted for a kid like me from a town like mine. I took the assignment as "make whatever you find fit" when it was meant to be "make whatever you find expand and explore." I capped my exploration at possible. I had always been a dreamer, but I had become a safe dreamer. A directed dreamer. Exploring what was realistic and acceptable.

If I am being honest, I wanted to be an enneagram three. They were everything I had convinced myself I was. According to the *Enneagram Institute*, **"Threes are self-assured, attractive, and charming. Ambitious, competent, and energetic, they can also be status-conscious and highly driven for advancement."**

This was me I would tell myself. Why was I testing as a seven. I had always been driven, energetic, ambitious, and competent. There was proof of all these things. This is who I was and this testing as a seven was just a fluke. Except it wasn't. I had been convincing myself it was, but it just wasn't. I had been forcing myself to operate like this for so long I couldn't even see who I really was anymore.

Every part of me wanted to stay true to what I had come to know over the last thirty years. My job now became taking time to continue uncovering where this was lost and where I saw my uncomplicated and true self showing up. What was true and what wasn't at this point was hard to decipher. If I was an enneagram seven, why didn't I feel like one? According to the *Enneagram Institute, sevens are* **"Extroverted, optimistic, versatile, and spontaneous. Playful, high-spirited, and practical, they can also misapply their many talents, becoming over-extended, scattered, and undisciplined. They constantly seek new and exciting experiences, but can become distracted and exhausted by staying on the go."**

When I read what a seven was, I felt my brain claim it like none of the other numbers, but when I looked for proof, I found very little except in the bad traits. I would go on to do more research on this topic. Like an obsessive amount. There isn't much I can leave alone when I get excited about it.

I found one author and content creator who spoke directly to my soul. She too is an enneagram seven (imagine). She wrote the book **The Honest Enneagram**. The author's name is Sarajane Case. This book broke down enneagram in the most digestible manner I had ever found. She talked about enneagram numbers when in stress. This was a beyond lightbulb moment for me. Once I finally accepted I was a seven, I needed to understand more about what that meant. In her book, she writes about how a seven's stress state puts them in an enneagram one operation. I was a little angry at the time because none of my swings, stress, or healthy states were an enneagram three, but I kept researching regardless.

This book became my enneagram bible. I sent this book to anyone who asked questions. It was and still is everything. It began to sink in that most of my life since age seven was operating in my stress state as an enneagram one. I haven't confirmed that this is possible with any enneagram experts, but from my own research that was what I believed happened. I was only willing to let out my seven when she was accepted, and when she was, I was everything and more that the definition of a seven describes.

According to the *Enneagram Institute,* **"Enneagram ones are conscientious and ethical, with a strong sense of right and wrong. They are teachers, crusaders, and advocates for change: always striving to improve things, but afraid of making a mistake. Well-organized, orderly, and fastidious, they try to maintain high standards, but can slip into being critical and perfectionistic. They typically have problems with resentment and impatience."**

All of this was well and good for a type one. But after carefully breaking down all of my foundational beliefs, I realized the things I had convinced myself I needed to care about I really didn't. They shook and tumbled to the ground unimportant to my core being. The things I had given strict order and rules to made me feel claustrophobic and anxious with every turn.

I read this book in the second season, but wanted to note it here because when I read it, all my permission to be my seven-ist self flowed in.

I was reading Jen Hatmaker's book *Fierce, Free, and Full of Fire - The Guide to Being Glorious You*. In her book she says this:

"Enneagram sevens, for example, were put on this earth to experience BIG YES LIVES. I parent a seven, and she once told me: "Mom, do you know what my greatest fear is? That, despite all of my dreams, I will end up working in a cubicle. I can't even watch office shows, they make me feel dark inside.""

When I read that, every inch of me took a gigantic leap forward into my actual being. There are people like me who feel the slightest pinch of containment and their skin can't help but crawl too. For an off paragraph and likely rather unimportant side note in this book, it hit me. The problem, it would seem, was not the broken dream at all as much as it was the mask I had put on as a result. I dreamt of bigness and came tumbling to an earth of humans ready to help me place myself nicely back where I belonged. Stuck, passionless, and miserable. Those things don't fit a seven, so I had to become something else. My life had told me I should want to become something else, so I did. My being could not wait to break free.

I just dropped more names and books than I am used to, so let me give you this asterisk. There was a time where I believed that I was sent here to save everyone. Honestly, it is a common stopping point for anyone who has learned something past the "average" human experience. Every part of my being told me to stop and bring people along. But the bigger part I was training myself to listen to my knowing said keep going. In the beginning, I shared all of the books and knowledge thinking that it would help, but the truth is I found everything I needed right when I needed it.

Just before writing this paragraph, I ventured out of my comfy corner chair up to my home office and retrieved Jen Hatmaker's book for the quote I was looking for. I remembered the exact location without a highlight or page fold. It hit me that hard. But when I went to find it, I kept flipping pages only to come up short. I put the book down and was about to write in (hold for Jen Hatmaker enneagram seven quote) when I told myself to just take a quick mental break instead. After I returned, I picked up the book one last time and opened to the exact page the quote was on.

I got better at this knowing. Days I used to spend searching for exactly what I needed to read turned into blissful wandering into corner bookstores (shout out Next Page Books in Cedar Rapids, Iowa who always lead me to my next needed stage of discovery) letting books, ideas, and expansions come to me. I no longer look, I let flow deliver. It delivers me to unexpected discoveries. Manifested in the most unexpected ways. So I stopped giving advice when I started believing in every person's innate ability to self-guide. Plus, I began to realize that what worked for an enneagram seven would likely NEVER work for a three.

At this stage, I discovered the importance of self-discovery. I began to become aware of how susceptible I was to those more powerful than me. So often, I would take their suggestions of a book, podcast, or transformative group and carbon copy their experience onto mine. I didn't want my work to be that for people. I wanted everyone to know and show up for what they knew to be true and embrace and believe in that more than anyone else. When I found who I truly was, I could begin to respect my own guidance. Before that, I couldn't, because what can one know if they don't even know themselves?

When I began embracing seven as my truth, I entered back into trial and error. I had more examination to do past the dreams and decisions I had made to date. I had to look at decisions I was living in and how I ended up there. It wasn't about just dreams anymore. It was also about the assessment of current reality.

I bounced back and forth in believing and confirming I had any say in that matter. I had kids, a house, cars, student loans, so it was easy to convince myself that jumping out of a cubicle and into my seven-ness was likely an idea that might put me out on the street, but now that I knew freedom was a part of this constant stirring and spinning, I couldn't let it go.

It made sense to most of what I would tell people about my job related to the creativity and freedom. I wasn't in a position to make a transition, but I could at least start accessing how one gets into position.

In the meantime, I was experimenting and trying new things inside my corporate office. There were things that might be more fitting of my newly uncovered seven self so I began to look to those. I started writing more consistently. I explored more options that might give me more room to create. Looking at options that would surround me in more optimism and positivity.

My podcast art is a yellow wall. When I picked it, I had settled on the name. I knew that I wanted yellow and canva was this new early adopter graphic design product that no one really talked too much about. This was 2019. Canva had some free images so I picked the coolest plain but not yellow backdrop I could find. I didn't put too much thought into it. It seemed rather similar to my choice of college. Mostly based on if their school colors included the color yellow.

The podcast was the first rung of the ladder. I have always been more intrinsically optimistic as an enneagram seven than most, so while this wall season was darker than normal, it was always painted with positivity. The wall was yellow.

Eventually, I would have to find a way to explore the beauty of darkness and light coming together to blip over the wall, but The Death Of A Dream was and will always be the one wall I had to stand in front of and find my way around. There were no optimistic words that could account for the actual work of climbing over. This was a scary choice when everything else had been safe. The title is dark and the artwork is light. A beautiful becoming of both. Enneagram sevens move to escape when faced with darkness painting the world an often untrue hue. I had to be yellow and face death to move past the wall.

Paint

Even when I knew I didn't want that, I could always paint the perfect picture. I always made this a joke. It was funny that I was so good at convincing people of things. So good that I made a career out of it. That was marketing to me. A chance to convey and move people where I wanted them and get them to do what I wanted them to do. I wanted to help whatever organizations bring their mission to the people and help make them see why this place, object, or piece of content was only going to change their lives if they got it from X.

When I was told this would be a good fit for me, I latched on hard. I also convinced myself it would be perfect. It was the safest and most creative choice that could be a fit for someone with my "skill set." I say that in quotations because that is how I always felt about my intelligence outside of sports. It was as if it wasn't really all that intelligent or useful at all where I lived. I was creative but living in a small rural community, marketing was a safe way to professionally explore creativity. So I labeled myself a corporate creative and did what I was told would be acceptable. I interviewed a lot of different people on my show and I feel like marketing is the scapegoat career for creatives. That is just usually the starter safe career choice for someone doing something on the side or longing to. That was me anyways. It seemed safe and someone acknowledged my worth there so I swam as fast as I could towards it.

When I discovered my enneagram number, it was the first time I started to explore whether or not this was all that fitting. Even if it fit before the podcast, I had no way to source my creativity. I was a number crunching marketing strategist, mostly just managing the people, decisions, and numbers, not creating. It was the safest choice I had been equipped to make.

I had no right to give up my need for safety, but I was starting to anyway. Once I knew more about myself, I was willing to put my guard down and start tapping even more into what it was that I actually wanted. I took on more creative opportunities at work and explored even more things that put a microphone in my hand. I liked the spotlight I had created for myself and I figured I could find more right where I was, so I did.

I wanted marketing to remain the fit. I had already torn up so much of my life, a career change just didn't seem needed at this point. I had experienced enough pain. So I found myself getting more involved and bringing more light to tables than I ever had before. I got asked to bring in a client I was working on a contract with to the biggest meeting of the year. This was a huge opportunity for me. That night I went shopping because, well, the huge opportunity and nerves I did not know how to handle left me with a tried-and-true comfort. Shopping. When I walked into Express, (it was a must due to extra long inseams) what was hanging right before me was the most epically yellow pantsuit jacket I had ever seen in my life. I looked at it and instantly knew. Since I still didn't quite trust that, I bought two outfit choices. I took a quick Snapchat poll and everyone who knew the real me agreed the yellow jacket outfit won. Old Hanna would have done what was right. New Hanna was working to do what was true.

I stepped on stage mouth full of words of passion for these two companies' intersection and potential growth together. I welcomed the client and exited. After the meeting was over, I stood out like a sore thumb. Actually, in the room full of monotone suits, the client that I had been working with and I matched in our blue and yellow break of the mold outfit choices.

While I was introduced as an up-and-coming employee of the company, I spoke to almost every single person that talked to me after. They assumed I worked for the other company instead of my own. The truth was that it was me. Maybe I had lived a life where monotone was a requirement up to that point, but my self-discovery had led me to remember I was more, needed more, and deserved more. I wanted color. I wanted freedom. I wanted to be me. I had driven my life to darkness which became dependent on this newfound light.

THE FIRST STEP
OUT OF THE
CYCLE

CHAPTER ELEVEN

Sure Steps

Steady

It has taken me years to learn this, but it does seem to be the case that if I am not actively creating something, then I am probably actively destroying something (myself, a relationship, or my own peace of mind). Big Magic - Elizabeth Gilbert

It amazes me to this day how true the above quote is. It took getting to phase three to realize that when I did not create an outlet for myself, I stayed stuck in my head, which stole my precious time and sanity. I was constantly looking for ways to draw up drama in my life. If things settled for too long, I made a big purchase or found something to blow up about. Nothing was off the table. In that mode, I could blow up at anything I may find unjust.

This made me someone people likely walked on eggshells around. That list of people likely included the core four within my own walls. Core four is the name of my stick together forever family that I have created. The core four loved me at my worst. They walked on an endless amount of eggshells for me and so I shall forever do the same when necessary for their growth as well.

Moving out of phase two and into phase three removed some of the shells. I remember the words tasting different as they left my mouth. Slowly but surely, I would find less and less words that resembled hate and drama. It was as if giving my words a purpose left me with less that I suffered without. I had much less room for drama, and not in the normal way where people claim to hate drama but constantly stir it up. There was no more room for me to hold for the wasted head space.

When I started, I wasn't sure where I would find the time, and this is where it came from. Chiming in on text message treads with an objection or throwing a hand up with words of disagreement in a meeting were not places I could be found anymore. It freed up more time than I even knew what to do with. The release of this constant drama loop gave me space to think clearly.

Finally, there was freedom to think. Along with that freedom, an ability to dream according to me. I had begun to build back my foundation, finding new things to fit right alongside the old. There was a light I could start to feel existing again inside of me. Always feeling it shine when I took time to do things I enjoyed.

For the longest time, I spent most of my time signing up for suffering I believed I deserved. Sometimes I would choose to suffer just because it at least got me attention I had been craving or it stirred up a reason to be mad. In case you haven't recognized it, I was very entertaining but I was not the good person I wanted people to believe I was. I was tired of living a lie to the world and coming home faced with the truth. I was draining the life out of myself and the core four. We were most tired when I was the most successful.

So, eventually, I hit rock bottom and everything settled and silenced around me. A moment I had been working tirelessly to avoid. It was the silence that allowed guidance to find me. After that, I could set the destination. I didn't know if any of this would stick, but I knew, if nothing else, at least I had written this list. This list of dreams was at least true to me and who I believed I wanted to be. Even if it was all wrong, it was all true.

I felt closer to myself than I had ever taken time to feel before. This happened in place of staying constantly surrounded by the crazy world of everyone and everything else.

I had released myself from the job of self-discovery, I over involved myself in the lives of others in an attempt to escape my work. But my life deserved to be lived and I deserved to be in it no matter how painful it was to release the weights holding me back. This was something no drama, purchase, or promotion would fix. I know, I tried.

So, I had to start finding time for these dreams. The constant cloud of drama no longer lingered in my free time. I filled this new found space with reading and writing. It used to take me a half hour to respond dramatically to a text or situation. Then another hour to vent to my sister and or husband. Then one more hour explaining and convincing everyone why I was right and whomever was on the other side was wrong.

Just like that, I found an extra hour a week, sometimes two to bring on something new. It took time to remove myself from this, but my sister, Heather, one day grounded and surrounded me with the reality that it just wasn't worth it. So, from that day forward, I worked to ingest as little drama as possible and even remove myself completely when necessary. Energy always better pointed towards the work of my dreams. The choice to be accountable for my actions was enough to give me some time back to work on them.

While I couldn't control people, I had control over my reaction to it all. I wanted to read. I wanted to write. I wanted to speak. I can't figure out why all of those things were just what sounded like the most fun. So I started to play with it all. I would grant myself time to just get in and get messy. Creating such big messes that I splashed on other people before I was ready to share, but it was light, it felt great, so I readily shared anyway.

Pretty soon, I found more time to devote to the expansion of the mess. My dreams took up the space of the lost art of drama because it felt so good to create with the misdirected energy that it expanded and grew into more time. I started getting good at five minutes a day. Just to write down a couple things in a journal. After about three months of five minutes, I felt ready to add more and take a little more time off my sleep schedule. I continued this cycle until I felt like I had added enough time for me to start my day with intention. My morning routine takes about three hours of uninterrupted focus, intention, and meditation. I just kept adding more minutes every three months until I got it right where I needed it to be.

The key wasn't some magic number. If I had started a three-hour practice the day I read it in a book, I would have quickly burnt out and got bored. The key is whatever I could consistently do. I could commit to writing my new dreams in a journal for five minutes a day when I worked full-time, was podcasting, and a mother of two kids under five. I had no more time and no reason to do more.

I enjoyed spending time with these dreams even if it was just in repeated written words. I liked the way they flowed from my fingers. I liked the way I felt when I took time to close my eyes and imagine with them as much as I could.

Rise

When I came home from my Rise conference in June 2019, I knew two things. The first was that Rachel Hollis had left us with the depressing acknowledgement that most people will come home on a high and do nothing all that different after all after the excitement of this moment wears off.

The second was that I FINALLY had dreams that both excited and nauseated me, and it felt fantastic. I came home on that high. I was hellbent to finally publish the podcast I had been drumming up audio bits for, sure that I would not be that person. She had also mentioned that as long as you are willing to keep going, anyone could make it.

I didn't know what it all would end up as, but I knew I could keep going. No matter what. The excitement and people all slowly faded into time and existence just like she said they would. I didn't feel the other part she promised most would. I could still feel my nauseating dream in me. So, I kept moving and eventually I told my husband these crazy dreams. I told him my word and my dreams. We sat in silence in the car driving to Sumner, Iowa.

After too much time had passed in silence, I said, "What do you think?" He said, "It makes me feel sick." I smiled the biggest smile of my life and responded with, "I KNOW, RIGHT!!! I THINK THAT MEANS I GOT IT RIGHT. I feel that too!"

Jordan knew in that moment that life would likely not look the same from here. He knew me better than I would even acknowledge me knowing myself. IT made him sick because he knew I was going to do this until it was done right and my way. Which meant what it meant for everything else. Time and willingness to put in the hours every single day. I knew that I would need to be the person who just didn't stop. Who found a way when and where there wasn't one before.

I really thought this would be the catalyst I needed to just start writing and start building out the dream. I did, but it never stuck like recording audio did. Eventually, I gave up writing because it seemed to suck energy from me. Podcasting never did. So much so, that I started pushing that to see if I could wear myself out in the work. While I do not recommend insane wake-up times as a fit for everyone and everything, I do recommend looking at where the energy repeats. As hard as I tried to exhaust myself, I couldn't. I could wake up every day no matter what feeling excited to get back on a microphone and create.

Eventually, just like I did with my morning routine, I would add in time and consistency to write. It was as if I had to lay out my thoughts in the show before they could become words on paper. It also just took time to believe in anything I had no reason to be pursuing outside of my imagined love. When it finally moved from imagination to actualization, I liked it even more. I found even more reasons to open up and explore further. Energy always repeating, daily activity creating more than ever before.

One of the things I am glad I did was the early release of expectations. I knew from the start that if I had to force my show down people's throats in order to find an audience, it wasn't meant for me. This allowed me to let go of any expectations that downloads, follows, and likes mattered that much. Which allowed me to silently and slowly learn a rhythm and flow that I could call my own related to my newly chosen outlets.

The truth is, I sucked. I am not entirely sure I still don't, but I still choose this and will continue. No matter what we choose, if it is just the start, we should let ourselves fumble, stumble, and fall.

I had shared more than I should have and let people in to see it early on, which should have stopped me because people are loving when it comes to dreams. They did their best to protect me from the seemingly unnecessary pain of sucking at something so bad, but it just was what it was. Pain I needed to experience to work through it.

I liked the idea that one day people would be able to trace all of the dots back and see firsthand day by day what it took. I let my imagination of one day standing on a stage (actually, I imagined I was in the crowd because I wanted to give the back row where I would have been sitting the chance to be VIP) talking about what it took to get here knowing they could go to the podcast and experience the pain of it all, not just the luster of this moment.

That floating vision kept me centered every day on the importance of capturing the mess that was becoming. I was actively learning with my audience. At one point, I realized I could go back and polish it all, but the vulnerability that was creating something I never knew would lead to anything is worth every minute of existence. So make it a mess. Finding myself took the active release experiencing these things I dreamt about. I brought them into my conscious state. I created something tangible. I gave myself space to test out what I thought I would enjoy. There was always a chance nothing fit, so I started with letting go of my plan or expectation and just let it be created in infancy.

I held myself up on visions of what the work would be when I had no proof of it being meaningful, life-changing, or even good. It still always felt better out than it ever did in, so I wrote most days, spoke almost every day, and brought stories and goodness into the world. I shall continue.

I found everything was a Google search away. That was both exciting and scary. When I wanted to turn my audio files into a podcast, I found a whole lot of guidance. More than I would ever need. I spent more time than needed spinning around in research trying to find the perfect guidance to apply to what I wanted to do. This became a new fun scapegoat pattern for me. If I was forever researching, I could avoid ever starting and always blame it on not finding the right platform. Since it was research-based, it seemed like a more accountable way of avoiding accountability. After researching for about three weeks and overusing my Google search bar and Facebook ads, I had to have downloaded a million and one free guides and watched a million webinars. This is great news, but I had to put a limit on it. I started limiting myself to two weeks of research so I would not stay forever inundated with ads attacking my every insecurity.

After two weeks, I forced myself to choose something and start working to apply it. If I needed more, I could find it, but not until I gave it a try. I would find that outside of a few first to the table influencers, most of the information was pretty much the same. I heard, "Find what works for you and do what you can to keep going." That is not what the ads were trying to convince me of. They had done a great job attempting to convince me they had the answers I sought and some secret path to everything I ever wanted. Unfortunately, they don't. Fortunately, we do, which is great because it will save us a lot of wasted time and resources.

Plasma

Somewhere in my commitment to myself, future audience, and family, I vowed to spend no money that I didn't make from either plasma donation or my entrepreneurial endeavors on this dream. I wanted this to be real. I didn't want there to be some sort of unspoken investor or leg up to my dream than I already had. So I committed essentially zero dollars. I know that I was already working well ahead of the curve with my dreams just having stability and the upbringing I did, so I did my best to remove the rest of the legs up. This commitment made not getting lost in the ad worthy expert advice easy. At zero dollars, I couldn't invest in it if I wanted to. Now no one has to follow this if it isn't necessary. I am not someone to look to more because I did it this way. This was just one of those things. I didn't want to bleed my family dry finding what fit for me. I also wanted to engage in the process of building something from the ground up. Investing money from our core four funds or family funds (neither of which existed even if I had wanted to) would have laid a slab of cement, and even as lovely as that sounded, I wanted to know every integral part of what I was building and how I did it. So I chose not to do it any other way. This did save me a lot of money that I'm sure I would have blown trying to find the next algorithm answer I would never be able to apply. What is great is that I had created a solid no strategy which led me to find what I needed in every single free offering, and there were a lot. I read between the lines of a lot of guides. If you make a similar choice for all things, you should know free is usually at the cost of time. That was great for me because I could find time, I could not find funds in the beginning. So I took what I could from everything and just did a whole lot of work.

There was an overwhelming amount of feedback voiced and unvoiced. It wasn't as much the reviews as it was the lack of them. As well as it wasn't the words as much as it was the lack of them. The silence that followed "I listened to your podcast" was almost strong enough to steal my breath and put me in an early grave, every time. Over time, I found resilience I wish I had started with. This came with the growing love of these outlets as a method for the expansion and full existence on this earth.

Words and silence etched so many painful periods of time in the beginning, but they never stopped me. This is where I was glad to have my ego still intact during the start-up of all of this. Short and silent responses I blew past with these shocking ego-based visions. It was enough to dismiss everyone and do the dang thing regardless. The words of distaste were easier to take. Usually, one hateful podcast recording cured me of the pent-up anger from that moment. The positive feedback would usually leave me running and creating for people as they popped up instead of staying true to my own journey and vision for this work. The good words left me blissful and wanting to serve and satisfy anyone who would acknowledge my existence in the podcast world. The truth is, neither good nor bad were all that helpful. So I became somewhat numb to both. Neither could matter. Neither could impact my creativity. I had to create for the sake of creating and I had to follow the storyline that mattered to me or it would quickly exhaust me and make me feel rather lost in the direction from the place I ended up following someone else's lead.

It was great to exist, but not at the expense of following someone else's direction. Creativity will always be subjective, so I always found it best to ignore the bad unless I found something worth fixing and embrace the good, but not let it drive. I found more ways to celebrate the good so I didn't find myself attempting to hold onto something not meant to be my muse.

CHAPTER TWELVE

Recycle

It's Ok

Now when I look back at my life, I see where I re-cycled back up to the top of the phases. Before I forced myself to sit down and think about it, I didn't give it an official name.

But I did think about it. A lot. It revolved around me feeling like I had failed at something again instead of feeling excited for something new to begin. There was always drama fueling the movement, change, or ending.

I realize now that some of the cycles moved rapidly in order to force a new start at a pace that would not have otherwise come to be. Some things came crashing down all together at once. After realizing how repetitive it all was, I could start to forgive myself for the guilt that came with the ending. I would also start to see the beauty in that part of the story as well.

I wasn't raised in a place where this understanding was readily talked about. Most people who cycled like this were known as dramatic, flaky, or never settled. So, when I planned my successful descent into adulthood, it always included staying somewhere for...forever.

I didn't want to be someone who was indecisive even though, truth be told, my plan to succeed seemed boring to me. In the eyes of everyone around me, staying equaled success, so I told myself to follow what people think fits and never move.

I started talking to people outside of my normal circles. These people always found my story quite comical. They would usually say, "Oh, that's just life. That's just how it works."

I would usually respond with a nod and "Yes, I know that now," but I didn't. It took this much work to find myself at this level of understanding.

Maybe it wasn't meant to be referred to as a mid-life crisis. It was just a constant cycle. I interviewed a lot of people on the topic of these phases. All of them confirmed the first two phases as a cycle that repeats throughout life. The people who took advantage of these cycles, moved easily through them seemed to be the ones at ease in life.

Being in the know took knowing people who knew something about the importance of experiencing a lot of things. I knew a lot of people who did a whole lot of the same thing for years and years and years. One career forever. From truths I had come to know those who didn't just didn't care much about their career. This is where I find this movement to be most important. I love showing examples of varied life choices. There was a track that was laid out for me, not only by counselors at school, but also by my family and societal suggestions. I never saw the routes that varied were also a track for success. I thought the varied and unsure route was a route of certain failure. So I avoided it. Had I seen more examples and known more people who had experienced something different and found success in life, I might have accepted this as a life that was good to explore. After finding more examples and meeting more people who had chosen this different path, I felt better. I had started accepting that variances were a well-lived life for me.

High Vibes

This was a whole new way to experience the world, and I saw that I needed new voices in my ears. This took breaking free from voices that would distract my newly known mindset. I loved the people I knew, but some of them couldn't come to this new place with me. Even when I wasn't sharing things with them, sometimes what they wouldn't say was enough to draw me away. So I had to cut ties. I knew that it wouldn't be forever, but I also knew that there were directions I could never go again with people. That the ways we bonded might have to evolve if I was going to stay. Some came along and some didn't. I never feared who would or wouldn't, I just paid close attention. Who was attracted where and when in the span of a month.

Once I got where I could see the energetic variances people were attracted to, I could figure out who was bringing me where. I had finally learned to value my energy, so much that I was no longer willing to let people steal it from me for their own use. I couldn't let them decide what the mindset would be if I was going to continue in these relationships. I would have to choose to bring the conversation up or exit when not able. My vision was too high to let people choosing low steal from me. If people wanted to be with me, they would have to raise to my energy.

Wavering without examples was something I felt early on. Not only from the example of varied life choices, but also high vibe existence. So I filled my ears with examples when I didn't have any in my stratosphere. This would put me on a high on days where I was able to tap into that energy even when just through a podcast or book.

The low in-between is what left me hanging. I had no one that could make up the gap between podcast episodes. It was one of the reasons I decided to record my show every weekday. I figured somewhere out there someone needed someone to walk through this with them. In case anyone was lost, lonely, and looking for someone like I was, I thought maybe I could be there. Even if the content was no good, at least it was always there and in forward motion. It wasn't as much what was being said as it was what was being shared. The headspace and energy shared with one another. Maybe just maybe my show could be that, because it was that for me.

Without this daily joining in on this upward movement, I would have stayed stuck. So it was work for me, but it was also for people who needed constant upward energetic movement to see the slightest change.

I was digging out of a low energetic hole, so once a week wouldn't have worked for me. It seemed so crazy at the time that personal journal podcasts were not a category. So I was just making something out of nothing. There was no example for what I was doing. The example which I made for myself was just relief. There was no template because it was a self-prescribed experimental trial that I was hoping would someday lead to a cure.

The goal at this point was to stay in this accountable state. Once I leveled up in this way, it started to become second nature. As I got better, everyone was a part of the coming up. I found myself bringing up conversations I would have. I also found myself completely avoiding people who couldn't find their own way there. Cutting the ties was sad for me because I tried to save so many people or at least bring them along in the understanding, but people have to choose that kind of life for themselves. There is nothing anyone can do to bring them over the threshold that is accountability.

Each person's moment to adopt this as truth is their own. Some get there and others won't, but I took a little too long hanging around and dropping my energy to help and hope they would change. They were never going to change, or they would somewhere down the road and maybe then we could come together again. I couldn't stay there to save them. I thought it was my job, but I realized it was anything but that.

Accountability is every individual's job and no one else's. It is kind of a part of the title. Imagine someone else deciding we should be accountable. It probably wouldn't go over well... I now understood this was not my work to do for them. Finding myself in conversations that were keeping me stuck in a mindset I worked every single day to escape started to interrupt my advancement.

The breakthrough requires extreme commitment. There is no exact timeline or schedule that will guarantee life changes as a result of the work. That is what is exhausting about it. I never knew if this would just be the weirdest thing I ever tried or if it would end up becoming something bigger, like the book I am writing right now.

This daily commitment to change who we are and how we are showing up should not be taken lightly. I wasn't afraid of the work. Just showing up was something I had become very skilled in. So the thought that I was going to be doing this self-development work every day forever didn't scare me at all. To me, it was the understanding that this is the work. It is getting back to the being. Doing was easy. That is just process development and execution. Being was what the work was all about. I wanted so badly to remember what it was like to mentally be where my two feet found themselves.

Silent moments grew in length and intensity. Opportunities to practice it more did as well. This helped me to see and intuitively know and listen to movements where cycles would come to an end. Even if this book would never become anything tangible or the podcast just stopped one day, it would have all been worth it because it helped me become. It helped me be. I could see myself in my life again. That was worth every sacrifice.

The anger that I kept feeling was an inconsistent bubble to live on. Something wasn't right about the way I was feeling. I thought everyone would be mad if I left them and did my own thing. I created a lot of stories in my mind about how people were against me. It helped fuel the movement.

I had to force this level of anger and discomfort in order to push my decision. My decision to finally do something different. My life was spent angrily speaking my distaste for everything about my life, but I never did the work to create action that followed. I wanted the best of both worlds. The world where I could talk and let out all of my pent-up energy and the world where I could live the life I could see when I closed my eyes. They couldn't exist together.

In order to get the life of my dreams, I would have to change my reality. That reality was not something easy to leave. After the dust settled on my initial announcement that I was going to do this thing, that I was going to chase a new dream...people just went right on not really caring.

A moment I convinced myself would change everything and make people hate me was rather anticlimactic. I was still in my drama creation phase, so I found some discomfort there, but looking back, if I am being one hundred percent honest, everybody went right back on to caring about their own lives instead of mine.

Just so we all are aware, what seems like a big deal won't be for long. The world is watching with one sleepy eye open. So I angrily, spitefully moved on past this moment. I tried to involve more drama than was there and then when everyone stopped looking and caring, I left. I left the anger behind, not for good, but I moved to the next phase. The look back was unnecessary. It was only forward from here.

What I know now is that the leaving, the people, the anger, and the spinning was the only way. I could not have created this any other way. Okay, that was dramatic. I am sure I could have...but here is the thing. We are all the result of our focus. So when I was focused on the bad and dramatic parts of life, guess what I created more of.

Focus cannot be fooled. It knows even where our minds are most of the time. Creating worlds of impossibility swirling around in our heads taking up every ounce of fuel we have left to make it all possible. The result follows what I put my mind to.

I spent a lot of time playing out instances in my mind that would never come to fruition. This is the reason the present moment was so vital in all of this work. It forced me to be right where I was, and right where I was didn't ever have issues. Even when it did, the problem passed into the next beautiful moment. Wonderful and terrible. This created a whole new way to exist.

In the beginning, I spent a lot of time in meditation and deep breathing. I understood how to call myself back to where I was. This took yoga and teachers on the topic. In the present, my frequency was mine to own. When I was in control of it, everything got better. I stopped handing over control to everyone else. This created a waterfall of goodness that could constantly wave and wash over me.

Full Heart

With each new learning and practice, I got better at controlling my power. I know this all probably seems like a Disney princess thing. Imagine controlling focus like Elsa discovering her powers in the movie Frozen. Initially it is nothing but pain, ice, and out of control emotions. So there will be a portion of the story where we retreat to an ice castle. Then people come and try to interrupt this newfound control we have discovered because they fear this power. So we use that strengthened power to almost kill some people and the entire ice castle tumbles as a result. There is a lock up moment where we must learn to control this new gift and find a way to make it work in the world we live in.

A captive no longer, even when everything is flurrying over, we find a way to make it all stop. We find a way exactly where we are to learn new things like love. That is where we finally discover our power. The world needs that person to come with full power back to this world. Even if it takes some time to bow out and be on our own, eventually they will want you back.

This part takes going full heart. I wanted to protect myself and go half-hearted into these new ventures. For a part of time, I did in fact. Eventually, it will be so life-giving the rest will get pulled in, so don't worry if we can't find it in ourselves to give it all right now. We will get pulled in.

I remember the specific time when I wanted the best of all the worlds. So I flirted with how that could work. I wanted to keep doing the show and having this release. I thought I would be like a pen name writer, but it would be pen name podcasting. I had put everything out without any noting or notoriety in hopes of keeping both lives alive. My personal brand is still a bit of a mess because of this very decision. Hopefully by the time you read this it will all be cleaned up.

I had decided I could do it all. I could trick myself into believing that I could make my job work with this newfound self. So I took on assignments that seemed more in line with where I wanted to go. I stayed here for a good amount of time. Trying to keep it all afloat and make it all make sense. Constantly reassuring my knowing that this could work.

Every part of me wanted to believe that, but my heart knew this was just false protection. This part is where I lived in-between real love and real life. I loved everything about the person I was becoming and the new life I was creating for myself. I lived in a reality that didn't match. The people changing was a start, but eventually everything had to follow for it all to line up.

My heart was in my podcast. My heart was now in my home. My heart was in the world I had taken control of creating. This didn't match what I was putting my focus on. This didn't match my real life for a while. I remember telling myself I just needed more microphones in my work world. I specifically remember asking for more opportunities to find my real life (which was my work) in alignment with these new things I discovered I loved. So I was given new things to focus my energy on.

People were trying to find reasons to make me make sense in this world too. I remember being on the phone with a boss. At one point, I remember saying, "I feel like the hype man in an industry that doesn't want it." It was hard to operate in this in-between, but reality...right. I kept looking for ways to make it work. My bosses did too. We all saw the value in who I could be there. I could fit, so I kept trying things on to find what that would be here. Living for a long time in-between real love and real life.

I had to keep building strength in myself in this new whelm. I didn't know that life could require a full heart. In fact, after volleyball ended, I put that heart of mine on a shelf. I rarely dusted her off. I wanted to protect her from ever getting hurt like that again. But the world didn't work well for me without it. It was cold and brash. It was spiteful and spinning. My life required my heart, so I brought her off the shelf.

Since it had been so long, it was a constant cycle of burning, breaking, recovering, and recycling. This is like a subphase. I found once I made it past my ego, I had to learn how to navigate the world in this way. It was like learning to walk as a child. My emotions were a mess. My world was a crumbly make up of who I could see when I looked at it with closed eyes.

Parts of this season were navigated with heart open and eyes closed. So I didn't venture or phase out for a while. I had to regain my footing. I had to discover what life could look like with my heart on my sleeve where I knew it belonged.

Finding what deserved my full heart proved to be where the burning took place. I gave everyone everything. I openly laid everything on the table, embarrassingly authentic in this new heart place. I found that it helped me to practice allowing people to leave or stay. If they knew everything, they could just decide. That became my new GPS. So I shared, unafraid of what it might cause people to decide about me. This is where the burning took place. I let people in who took that openness and used it against me and given the chance I would not take any of it back. Those experiences were what allowed me to see the worth in my full heart and to not just give it away. It was a sad but necessary burn. I broke every time. My whole heart broke.

Everything about what I had learned told me to engage my entire heart, but I would think maybe they didn't know this. Maybe they had not experienced what I had come to know to be true. Maybe they lived in a better place or maybe I was doing it wrong.

Either way, I would break and build myself back up again in my ice castle away from the world. I was still in my real life, but not really. My real life hurt my real love. So I stopped letting it out. I stopped letting my heart lead. I would recover. Then I would go out to the world broken but still better. I would spend my free time recovering with things I loved.

Once I felt healed, I would work up the strength to re-enter the world with my full heart again. Burn, break, recover, re-cycle. Staying here was hard to experience, but it made me more sure than ever that I wanted my heart in the work of my life. It would force my hand at deciding to live full heart no matter what it took. No matter how much pain. No matter how many times I got burned. I was going to live my life with my full heart because my dreams required it.

CHAPTER THIRTEEN

Regain Control

Magnet

I used to start my day magnetized to my phone and the constant need to render drama. I would wake up hungry for what was going to put me center stage the rest of the day. Hungry for who and what I could talk about that would let me talk as much as possible. Hungry for people to find me the most interesting. That took an ear to the ground at all times, a news feed, and socials. This was exhausting and exhilarating. Until I recognized how it was depleting me, I had believed it gave me life. I believed it gave me purpose.

That hamster wheel is hard to get off because once I was the source of information, people looked to me for it. They thought it was weird or something had gone wrong when I didn't offer it. This took the most time. I was hardly perfect at this. I stayed in the loop for a long time.

This isn't meant to be a conspiracy theory book, but I will lay this out from my past life in marketing. There is enough data on us to build our life and interests ten times over based on our daily activity online. The media has more information at their fingertips than they ever did before, and they haven't even started to use it to its full potential. I say that just to point out this part isn't easy. If leaving the people I knew and loved for a little time to let life settle was hard, this was even harder. Bad news is everywhere. The media and social networks know we can't resist. They knew it fed my ability to feel important that day. So it fed me the entire spectrum of bad.

The cool thing is, just like I decided to start recreating my life, I could also decide to create a better feed. It took time. Facebook wanted to send me over the edge and involve me in endless online disputes according to what I care about most, but I decided one day it felt better to live outside of the drama. It was a Wednesday morning and I posted to a group about a copied hashtag that infuriated me. The hashtag had presented itself as one letter different from the one that we were trying to build up and I had almost liked and shared it. So I took to the group posting a warning about it to everyone. The group rallied hard. They got the hashtag reported it was a swirling thread of vengeance.

I felt super anxious the whole time it was going on. The moderator finally came on and laid it all out. She would go on to say basically the internet is going to do things like this and everyone has a right to their approach and opinion. She handed out a big ole' settle the F down and do the work. I felt even more anxious about the whole thing than I did before. In that moment, the world went fuzzy and I settled unconsciously into my head, walking around outside of what had just happened. It was there that I came face to face with the decision to stop creating and living in drama. The feeling I had wasn't worth the payout. Even if the moderator had come on the page and congratulated me, crowned me queen of hashtag hunting, I realized it still wouldn't have been worth what I felt all the moments leading up to the decision. The rush of posting or something seemed fun but it was like I became the owner of the result and I realized I didn't know why I would voluntarily sign up to be that. Someone else should own that piece should they so choose.

From that point forward, I was going to do less. Over time, the need to be owned by the dramatic lessened. I would start my day filling my head with great things instead of the opposite. It meant intentionally tapping out of my normal routine of staying close to a screen.

I want to point out that every piece of media we have access to is amazing. The ability to stay close to it all is great. It is all about timing for me. If I can start my day filling my soul with what it needs to maintain a great vibration through the day, then I can pretty much stay in control. I am great at directing my day when I get to set the tone. A simple start is all it takes. I just focused on doing one thing really well and watched as more followed.

While I didn't know it then, I was very much establishing a good vibrational practice. I was setting my expectations for the day. I used to just let the day run me, following the highs and lows as if it was completely out of my control. I realize now that it was not.

Eventually, I grew even stronger in this, but I started with just testing it. Seeing where my day took me on days where I was intentional about the tone set. Comparing them to days where the day ran me. Days where the drama led. Intentional days always felt better. Those days there was no undertone of anxiousness.

When I started to see this, I was willing to give more time to it. You should know, and you might already, that I am slightly obsessed with do and review. I don't like to spend time in dreamland for long. It is and always has been in the movement for me. This isn't a new skill. This is a pet peeve. I don't believe in dreaming if there is never doing that follows. It is rather pointless.

Review, do, repeat is the rhythm for me. I decided that the only way I could know is to stop dreaming and start doing. I dreamt of being a writer and had never written a word. So, I got better at the review and not just my doing review, which I had kind of had down by this time.

The being review was what I focused on now. I would come home and think about what energy I had maintained and created that day. I would piece it all together. Sometimes this would come to the podcast as I got this right or I was completely thrown off by this. Over time, I found patterns. I saw where and what impacted my ability to act as my best self. The review of it all became the process that kept it all moving forward. Without the review, I think I would still have been stuck standing where I was.

This meant society was no longer running my life. I had taken control for once and for all. I was the owner of my continued vibrational pursuit. I was in control of it all. This was different from anything I had done before because the focus had changed. The focus became my energy. The focus was on me and what I could own. I could create the life I wanted from here.

As I continue to perfect the energy understanding, it is no perfect science, just an imperfect commitment to an ever-evolving practice. Since society no longer had a say, I was free to move about and do what I wanted. Create the life I saw fit with who I was in each given moment.

As I write this right now, I remember how fearful I was of this moment and how much less nervous I am not to trust it, but I had decided that is how it works. When I am actively creating the life I want, the world can react and create accordingly. When I am in movement of my dreams and beliefs, I am in a better vibrational state. The world reacts to what I decide instead of the other way around. This was a movement from consumer to creator, and that vibe just hits all the way different.

Flow

One day I woke up, silence fell all around me. After doing the review process for long enough, I started to understand what was aligned and what wasn't. It set me up to forever stay in awareness. Always watching what was contributing and what was taking. It was as if the world had been freely flowing all around me and I had woken up and pressed slow down mode. Things began moving in slow motion all around me.

Understand that this pace would have been enough to send me off the deep end not too many months ago. Now it was like I had a leg up on everyone. This gave me the ability to review and pick through. To fully feel those around me like I never had before. The day the world went silent and I felt things around me cascading into my life at a digestible pace. This was my taking control and it was just allowing things to flow. I stopped taking on things that would disrupt my peace because I finally knew what peace was. It was hard for me to know what would or wouldn't disrupt before allowing myself to fully feel it. Silence surrounded me and I sought it as well. I couldn't escape the slowdown if I wanted to at this point. It became the better version of who I was. I felt like I was in a movie where I could fast forward and slow motion every piece of my life willingly. This is what choosing the present moment did for me. I started soaking in what was good and lived in what was bad as well, but I was always there full person. Full heart.

I gave myself full permission to be mysterious to those who have not taken time to get to know this new version of me. Every part of me wanted to over explain what I had gone through, not only to attempt to teach but also to bring people along with me. I would quickly realize not everyone wants that and most importantly not everyone needs that to feel whole. So, I committed to the mystery.

While I was living life out loud on my podcast, and soon to be books, I was also very committed to only letting people in who decided I was worth exploring. Most people grew rather disinterested. There isn't much drama in the evolution of a human being. It is a slow methodical commitment to a process that is very much discovery of the unknown. I didn't know who cared, and I stopped caring too. If someone happened to stumble upon who I was and decided I wasn't for them, it kinda felt like the leg work of having to decipher all of that was already done. I liked being able to live out loud and let people decide versus my previous life, which included a whole lot of catering to as many people as possible. Those who didn't do the work to get to know me missed out. This process helped me find my worth, which allowed me to stand for who I was and who I let it be. My amazingness saved for a select few.

The problem was that I had no dreams, which was a major problem, but that was not all of it. It was a problem because it kept interrupting my ability to let my life flow. Life flow was the problem, not as much what I was or wasn't doing. Without having a focal point, my life sort of operated like a really crazy roller coaster. Weaving in and out and up and down. It was nauseating and not in an exciting way.

This understanding would soon start to level out my life. It gave me something to focus on that was outside of the things that drove me crazy, which made all of those issues that used to be debilitating rather uninteresting. I found what I was working towards much worthier of my time.

It did not matter if I had written tough dreams or easy ones, my life was craving something to sink its teeth into. When my dreams died, I just let my life happen. The key to finding flow is setting the direction. That is really all it takes. Then I just didn't let myself off the hook for the things I said I wanted. Keeping a telescope and microscope view. Allowing myself to see the big vision and committing myself to do the daily work to bring it to life. That started as small as necessary so long as it was movement. I laid my dreams out in my head and then moved them to paper. I spent time with them. I let them in and I let them out.

I knew what I wanted and let myself operate according to what it was that I wanted from life. I got into a flow state when I had an exact list of what it was going to be for me. It wasn't whether or not the dreams excited me, it was whether or not they existed at all. So I started focusing on what it was going to be for me and things followed like I could have never dreamed. I realized I had to gamify life to keep myself interested in it. No matter what it was. Saying what I wanted was vital in establishing a new frequency. Doing the work helped create flow.

Here is the deal...dreams are amazing and scary. People who share the things they want in their lives amaze and inspire me every single time. I love giving people a safe place to say the thing for the first time out loud. As they grow stronger in their relay, it is like it solidifies right in front of them. There is not a more beautiful thing for me to experience in this life. Dreams are sacred. I know firsthand how hard it can be to say it and I also know how important it is to find someone to say it to. What is scary is the unknown reaction, and depending on what you are looking for, it can throw the entire dream thing for a loop.

I love to just celebrate the conversation knowing how much strength it takes to even say it out loud for the first time. Attacking something in that vulnerable of a state is heartbreaking. I have lived both existences. The dream hater and the dream lover. Dream lover fits much better. All that to say, it is one hundred percent okay to just want something. There does not need to be a resume of reasons to want it. There does not need to be a lifetime of achievements, courses, or education.

Real Want

There was just the decision and me. No real reason, just real want. Over time, I could start connecting the dots, but in that moment, everything I wanted made the LEAST amount of sense to me. I wanted to speak EVERYDAY (I knew not a soul who had done this, I had no degree in journalism or broadcasting, I had no platform or audience, I lived in a town of about 1,700, only a handful of which I knew).

I wanted to write FIVE books (I hadn't written a word that was not assigned by a teacher, I had no degree in journalism or creative writing, I lived in Iowa, not exactly the meca for publishing houses). Those two things made no sense and there was a list of eight more things that made even less, but they were mine.

When I started going after these things, I got a lot of raised eyebrows. This is why it's best to just remain mysterious in these first couple phases. I found myself filled with reasons, words, and excuses to make sure that I had a resume to back up these dreams, but it was pointless. Even more pointless was my attempt to bring people along with this belief I had.

I tried too. I found myself on stages where I encouraged just doing what you wanted. That was a poorly reviewed speech. People wanted specifics. They wanted exact answers and specifics I didn't have the answer to. I sat there and defended my poorly thought-out hypothesis that I optimistically assumed would not be questioned. It made sense to me. We should just do what it is that we want to do. Eyebrows shot up. It was as if what I was saying could never be true. I sat after for a while, saddened not because my reviews were less than wonderful, but sad that this wasn't an assumed truth people had come to know.

People were skeptical of my presentation because proactively acting out of truth was seen as far more belligerent than living life in reaction to the world. I was asking people to dream visions they may have never let themselves see. The demand was just too much and about six steps ahead of what could be comprehended. There was too little proof of my approach and too much proof of the other.

Having lived my life in a state of flux for forever, it was hard to believe that I would ever settle into an even operational flow. I had adopted this as my truth. There could not be evenness as I was just meant to be uneven. I had been told my brain just worked this way and there was nothing that could be done to fix it. There wasn't, but it wasn't broken either. It was beautiful and divine when in the right environment.

One day, I found a way to bring it all together, but my brain still needed days to wonder and be free. I have to create tools that could wind within the rhythms of my mind. It took so many things to get to this place that I still have no idea what it was that brought me here, but I do know that the flux settles.

I was afraid that sending my life into upheaval would disrupt my being forever. It was the only thing that could have ever fixed it. The forced instance of surrender brought me further than I could have brought myself. I didn't deserve a life that left me weaving in and out of existence. I wanted to be here and leave whatever mark I was meant to. Big or small, the significance of doing anything at all was enough for me. I could never unknow what I know now and that was enough to save me. My life had already placed me close enough to my rock bottom. Did I really "need" to take that further? Was this a requirement of this work to understand and engage myself directly into the flux with hopes that it would somehow cure it? It was a crazy approach. I knew then that I could not fear the edge. I had to just step off.

I am to the point of understanding that being is the key here. Similar to this idea that flow is more important than the actual dreams. I always found myself clinging so tight to the things I wrote down, nervous that they may leave if I glanced away even for a second. I had the tightest grip on the things I wanted and the direction I would take to get there. Even though I was taking action towards my dreams now I lost all flexibility.

This tight grip had directly impacted my desire to continue to pursue at times. So I found it best to let go and let flow. To find myself floating above it all, not forcing any one experience over the other. Knowing that when I show up as my fullest self, I get aligned opportunities to change the world. I find myself focusing on where I can be. Usually surrounded by silence. This has followed me throughout life.

When I met my now husband, I found myself for the first time settling into silence with another human that I had never known. I could not have verbalized that at the time but now I know. Places I belong include places where silence and enthusiasm flow equally through the veins of existence. When the balance is off for too long, I now know that I have to take time to recalibrate and set it all equal.

I find it quite comical that I avoided silence for so long assuming it would be the death of me when all throughout my existence it had given me life. Being is silence that doing can't outwork. It is not everyone's requirement, but it is mine. May I forever find myself in places and surrounded by those I can take up equal parts quiet and adventure. Neither of which exhausting or out-playing the other. Finding my life in an equal state, experiencing the world in its fullness, never trying to escape silence meant for the thread of my life holding all of it together.

CHAPTER FOURTEEN

Re-Define

Lost mind, found heart

It was as if I had lost my mind, which almost made me stop everything I had started.

I wanted to figure out my dreams to save my mind and soul... the things I was doing seemed to be driving my madness further into the ground. Every part of me wanted to stop. While I could feel myself spinning further into my mind and madness, I also felt a strange sense of direction that was a force pulling me forward. My high and low states were getting worse at about six months into the work and I almost called it quits.

Luckily for me, one light reached out. They said they found something in themselves they wouldn't have discovered without this work. So every second that I wanted to quit and put a cap on the work because it was driving me more mad than ahead, I kept that person as a focal point. It was enough. This was the first needed validation of my work. Comments without which I would have never continued. I would have never found my story while living it. All of this would have ceased to exist and there is a chance I would have dimmed myself completely out of existence in my own life.

I want to make a special note to pass on how important these lights are in the world. If you are that light, never stop telling those encouraging stories back to people. Your very existence changes the world. There is never a light burning too bright that couldn't benefit from more. Even though I wanted to stop, I couldn't help but feel like I was seeing life for the first time. It was as if my life got a new lens. Things that simply guided my black and white world turned gray. This perspective was both unnerving and enticing. A rapid new way of seeing the world unfolding right in front of me.

Fading

Every part of me was fading.

I felt myself merely existing. Each day passing as just another unexplained miserable motion. Not seeing any worth in what I was here to do. Finding myself fading out of existence in my perfectly wonderful life. I was stuck in the middle, motionless. No one could have known that this was how I felt. I felt guilty for feeling this way considering I never had it THAT bad. Which was true, but that truth didn't fix how I felt.

It was a devastating way of looking at the world. There was happiness I just couldn't seem to assign to any parts of my story even when it was right there. Time spent searching and hopelessly longing for something to come along and snatch me out of this moment. Nothing came. There I was, the poster child of imaginary happiness. Toxic positivity running through my veins and passive-aggressively out of my mouth. It was all a lie. A lie that the more I told the faster I faded.

When the success sent the lie spinning all around me, it took off and became something bigger than I could keep control of. It looked like me. My life looked like something I had created, but it was a delicate shell, one that with slightest touch could come crumbling down around me. Eventually, I would talk out the lying, spinning spitefulness I knew was untrue. After breaking down the walls of lies I had built my life on, I threw a rock at the window and watched as the walls came crashing down. If I was going to do this, it was going to have to be authentically me.

From there, I would walk backwards to go forward. I had never really thought much about what had gotten me where I found myself. My life presented itself as a rather unalarming childhood experience. Nothing all that traumatic that I can remember happening to me. So I glazed over it as if there was not a thing there. It was fine, so I moved on.

While I didn't like combing through it all because I was scared of what I might have to deal with if I did find something, I also knew that was how I ensured I didn't build a glass house again. The words and walls needed to be built on a knowing that I could only find when looking back at where I came from. I have to remember what my life was actually like in order to remind myself what it was like to exist again. To remind myself how enjoyable my life was when I was in it. It was the only way forward for me. Obviously seems counterintuitive, but it's the only way to remember who you were before the world got in the way. I needed to remember what I had left behind when I left myself to perform for the world.

Forward looked like tiny steps into the unknown. My venture backward wasn't even on sure footing, but I found that the smaller and seemingly less significant, the more willing I was to commit. Overwhelming myself wouldn't work. I didn't have time as it was. Belittling myself wasn't the ticket either. Hating myself to work harder just didn't stick for long enough to be effective.

There was no one responsible for holding up what I wanted.

No one assigned me to find happiness in my life. So I only did what I could to discover it on my own. To take words I had always been passive-aggressively sharing online and actually start applying them to my life. If I was unhappy and no one knew, how do I know the rest of the world wasn't suffering too? Was there a way to intuitively carve a path back to myself? I couldn't help but try to figure that out. From five minutes to three hours, I would find my way back, but it all started with tiny steps. Tiny, rhythmic, uncertain steps into the unknown.

More than anything, I wanted to create a better life for the core four. I didn't want my two daughters to one day wake up suffering in their own story because of a life I or society had projected onto them. I realized there weren't words that would teach them what living proof could.

A few short months after finding my limiting belief vibration of thoughts constantly weaving my mind together, I decided to do something for my girls. I decided I would build beliefs I wished I had built into me so strong and fierce that they never question them like I had with my lies. But I wanted to route theirs as truths.

I picked the three most important beliefs I wished I had as a structural belief and ended it with a challenge. My main goal was to keep them from adopting anything but these as truth. I grew up questioning my beauty every single day of my life. My intelligence came into constant question after the first grade. In fact, I completely resigned from the idea that I would ever be seen as smart. The one thing I knew of was my strength, but I didn't hold it up as a valuable trait. I constantly made it more approachable and less intimidating. I was told I could change the world but stripped my own voice and ability to do so.

So, every night before my two babies go to bed, I kiss them and lay the same three beliefs to rest with them: You are smart. You are strong. You are beautiful.

Then I let them voice the answer to the question What are you going to do? Change the world.

I believe that we change the world by staying true to ourselves. I like to pose this as a simple daily commitment because it lessens the intensity of it. The world changes through steps that are seemingly insignificant. The world changes from ideas that start as nothing but a spark and grows into something burning desire. The world changes by humans acting in their truth, in their individual identity.

I had been tucking my babies (then two and five) in nightly like this for a while, and one night everything changed. My two-year-old turned to me after tucking her in, kissed my forehead, and said to me, "You are smart, you are strong, you are beautiful. What are you gonna do?" I responded with "Change the world."

It wasn't until that moment I began to realize the impact of it all. This work was for me and it was changing everything. My kids could feel the cascade of a parent coming back fully into their light and back into their lives. I will never forget the stumbling, but knowingly strong words my daughter laid on my forehead that day. They could already see how I was changing the world around them and the response to change the world was something they could see their mom and themselves setting out to do.

After that night, I started closing my show with that blessing. If my kids and whoever comes to know me is left with nothing else, they should always know I believe this to be true to every single person's core set of truths. You are smart. You are strong. You are beautiful. What are you going to do? Change the world.

There was something inside me pushing me to this knowing that this was not who I was meant to be. It was rather sneaky, usually disguising itself as anxiety, depression, or anger. I found myself waiting for someone to come along and discover that truth buried deep inside. Like someone was going to come along, unlock, and unleash it. I wanted to love, but it was buried in hate.

In the Disney movie Moana I was Te'ka. Angry at the world because they couldn't see who I really was. Angry at myself because I felt powerless in my ability to unlock it. My beliefs had deemed me powerless, a knowing built so deep in my soul it would put the fire out on anything that started to burn.

Scared to show the world who it really was because of how it was hurt in the first place. Heart on sleeve, eyes wide open. So I walked in this world in a cover of ash never believing in my own intelligence or beauty. Passing all strength off with quick wit.

Slowly covering it all up with ash. Leaving my flames burning, but not brightly.

I knew deep down this is not who I was. There was no Disney princess coming to return my heart. I had to find my way back to it. The journey was long and I wanted to throw myself overboard many times, but the universe, or ocean if we are keeping the Moana narrative alive, kept bringing me back aboard.

Every time I lost faith or found myself asking for the next answer, there it was. As the ash started to fall away, more power followed. I feel like I always knew who I was meant to be, but the visions didn't line up with my reality. So it was easier to cover my existence in lies keeping me from getting burned ever again. I knew my life required my heart on my sleeve to be me.

All the Powers

Getting past the phases takes a whole lot of patience with little expectations. The cool thing is that every single higher power has your back. This is advanced knowledge that I wished I had trusted more fully in the beginning. I wasted a lot of time questioning whether or not it was all going to be okay. Whoever and however you assign those forces, just know they got you.

I like to explore higher powers as openly as possible. Since there is no certainty on the subject, I feel better keeping it gray.

Feel free to assign as black and white as you see fit. But whoever, however I cannot deny the powers above making this world turn. Power so scientifically unknown it makes my head spin. I have come to love it, and at the start of this work, it was yet another thing to blame. I believe in utilizing all powers in the work of your dreams. I figure we might as well put all the powers to work for us. I know I needed them all.

The way I found my quickest path to success was just accepting and loving exactly where I was at in the process no matter what. Again, something I had to learn a whole lot about before being able to write something about. I suffered for longer than necessary. Truth be told, it was a self-inflicted wound. I could have been happy, but chose to dangle it like a carrot in front of my face. Instead of just handing happiness over, I made myself keep it hanging for no reason at all.

If I had given in and let myself experience happiness I had always been deserving of, chances are good that the powers could have aligned sooner. But I held happiness as a goal and it isn't meant to be that.

It isn't something I couldn't have held all along. The fact that I had woken up that day to breathe a breath should have been enough reason to give myself the dang carrot. Everything I had was enough. I was capable of experiencing happiness according to my own assignment. Again, there was no one and nothing coming to grant that wish. I had to decide to make happiness a part of my story. I had to surrender to every part of who and where I was to discover happiness weaved into the fabric of my entire existence. It was always meant to play out this way. I didn't have to wait for vacation, a raise, or a major contract. I could be happy right here and right now with all that I had made it through and all that I was already doing.

At thirty, I thought my life was crashing down around me. By thirty-two, I realized it was a necessary step in the process and willingly threw the rock at my glass house. The death of my dream was never meant to be the end. It was meant to inspire a new beginning, but I saw it as a depressing reroute in life.

I lied to myself and said it was all meant to be less and then took on that unfitted assignment. I had accepted my bigness as assigned and that was why it didn't work out. I had to get to this moment, had to live this story out loud to bring these words to the world. Most importantly, to bring these words to me to discover and draw a path forward for myself.

This is the map I had thrown away at seven years old. I gave up my right to decide and found my life withering away as a result. I was waiting for happiness that was not guaranteed.

When I realized that I wanted to use my voice to tell stories, I knew I needed to change. One of my favorite motivators Dave Ramsey says, "Money will only make you more of what you already are." So I went to work to change the things I was before the abundance could bless me with more spite, hate, and darkness. Abundance was headed my way on the path I was on, so I ran from it.

I couldn't imagine a life that spread my hate further. I couldn't imagine my soul darker than it already was. I knew that it didn't have to be the end I promised myself it was. That passion, love, and enthusiasm for life could fit somewhere. It didn't only belong on a volleyball court. It belonged with me. I had to find where all of that greatness was left and go back to collect it. I had to bring it along to infuse in this new life I had made true. This fit better than anything I had ever experienced so I had discovered the death was in fact a rebirth.

Persistence

This is a letter I wrote to myself on the day I assigned myself control of my life.

June 15, 2019 - RisexMinn

Dear Hanna,

I am your persistence. I am the part of you that never gave up and this is what I want you to know. You are so strong and smart. You have never once given up and you have always found a way. You cannot and will not be stopped, just like you never have been before. You are the person you have always dreamed of. People and challenges have been put in front of you with purpose to show you that purpose. Your purpose is what it has always been and YOU have what it takes and YOU always have. YOU have never stopped and you never will. YOU make your life happen...NO ONE ELSE DOES EVER AGAIN!

From here on out I promise to:
Stop attaching myself to someone else's agenda for my life.

Sincerely,
Your Persistence

This was always meant to come to life this way. It is all etched everywhere I looked. Played out clearly like a scene from a movie when I closed my eyes. My reality didn't line up until my beliefs did. My reality couldn't line up until I re-awakened the soul I had put to sleep. I had to remember the warmth of yellow. I had to regain the strength in my untrusted knowing.

There were parts of me that had been burnt out for such a long time I didn't know if they would ever come back. This is the story of how I brought myself back into the storylines of my reality.

As I sat back and watched my life and importance fade into nothing but carpools, deadlines, and meetings, I found a burning desire to exist as more than that. For myself and everyone around me.

While it seemed to be a strange road, it was the only truth I had come to know. Everything in my being needed yellow. Everything in my knowing needed expansion. Somewhere they all etched together to bring the world this. Everyone in the world can benefit from just one more light finding its way. This book, my podcast, and anything else I come to do in this world is a result of the expansion of me choosing light.

In order to find my way from the death to the rebirth, I had to hand my life over to curiosity that I once trusted as a child. From there, my intuition could lead me back to my true path. It is okay to let your light fall like seeds to the earth never knowing what they end up growing.

That is the persistence of yellow.
That is how you change the world.

ACKOWLEDGEMENTS

I have always wanted to write a book. I was certain I could easily accomplish this feat but it took me six years to bring this work into the world. Every word painfully lived first, committed to memory, spoken on, explored, and brought to the written word. This work would not be possible without all the people who showed up first to see what I couldn't. I only show up in this work because these brave souls saw me fading and chose to love me back into existence. They chose to walk with me in their light to guide me back to mine.

Every drop of love to the core four. To my husband Jordan who saved me the first time that I was disappearing from this life. He chose me and that changed everything, he keeps choosing me, and that empowers me to change the world. To Emerie, who found me when I had forgotten how to exist. To Baelor, who reminds me why I need to exist.

I have to take time to thank our family who shows up and goes along with it all. Showing up to babysit, fold, edit, share, like, and buy things they don't even ask to understand and help anyway. They showed up with patience and love even when I didn't and never gave up on who they knew I could be.

Shout out to my beautiful friends who lived through their own dream deaths right along with me and found their footing when I could not. Their strength helped guide me to this place. Guidance which I could not have lived without.

I need to take time to thank Erika who early on confirmed what I was feeling and gave me confidence that my words could find a place to help in this world. If she had not taken the time to give me that initial spark none of this would exist.

I feel so blessed to have tools like Fiverr to hire help for publishing my book. I knew that the world would have to create tools for me to do this, I just never realized it would be so easy to find and use. Shout-out to all the creative support I found there to help move this project over the finish line.

The teams of people who let me experiment which inevitably led me to this work I owe you so much. Every step you let me grow into who I was supposed to be and still loved me when I showed up as less. I was blessed to coach athletes early on and still find myself blessed with athletes and organizations who buy into my ability to build teams and humans.

Last but not least, thank you to my parents who have always had blind faith in me my entire life. I could not have been raised better in this life. Everything I do now is possible because of the world they created for me where they dared me to dream unapologetically.

* 9 7 9 8 9 8 9 0 5 0 9 3 2 *